PRAISE FOR HELEN

'Comical, affecting, honest and a[...]
got a beating heart.' – *North & S[...]*

G000162485

BONO THE RESCUE CAT
'Helen Brown is a great telle[...]. –Radio Arabella, Munich

TUMBLEDOWN MANOR
'A fun deep-dive into Down Under, complete with colorful characters, kooky animals and a strong woman getting her groove back. A wonderful book.' – Amy Reichert, author of *The Coincidence of Coconut Cake*

'Delightfully written, very charming and laugh out loud funny.' – *Weekend Herald*, Auckland

CLEO
'One of the most moving books I've ever read.' – UK's largest book club, Books Direct

'An epic, genuinely moving, funny and uplifting.' – Witi Ihimaera, author of T*he Whale Rider*

'Helen Brown's remarkable memoir took me on a journey that threatened to break my heart, and right when I thought I couldn't possibly bear to read another word, I realized she didn't break my heart – she opened it.' – Beth Hoffman, author of *New York Times* bestseller, *Saving Cee Cee Honeycut*

AFTER CLEO CAME JONAH (JONAH in the USA)
'A must read. Five Stars.' – *The Lady,* UK

'I adored this memoir to the point that I could not put it down.' – Kelly McLean, NZ Booksellers

'A pleasant and moving story of love and identity among mothers, daughters and felines.' – Kirkus Reviews.

ALSO BY HELEN BROWN

DON'T LET ME PUT YOU OFF

How to survive suburbia

HELEN BROWN

For our daughter, Katharine,
who solved the maternity hospital problem
by being born at home.

With fondest love

First published 1981
Revised and extended 2019

ISBN: 978-1-0763238-0-4

Cover design by Deborah Parry

CONTENTS

FOREWORD

My knees turned to playdoh when an advance copy of this book landed in our letterbox. I was twenty-six years old and we were living in Homespun Grove with two little boys. It seemed unbelievable that my quirky newspaper columns had been collected into a real book. I clutched it to my chest and hurried inside out of the wind with our dog, Rata, snuffling at my heels.

Sitting at the kitchen table, I counted the pages. It was a short book, but a book no less. Though it'd been written for a small New Zealand readership I was gratified when Ita Buttrose, then editor of the Sydney *Sunday Telegraph*, ran *Don't Let Me Put You Off* in extract form over two months.

Revisiting these pieces from the seventies and early eighties is like watching a canoe headed for a waterfall. I guess it's the closest I'll ever come to meeting my younger self. She's wounded, pig-headed and quite funny at times. Looking back at her across the decades, I understand her vulnerability and frustrations.

If only I could reach out and reassure her things will be okay. Then again, there is a shadow hovering over these pieces. Not long after this book was published, our older son, Sam, was run over and killed at the age of nine. Our family plunged into the abyss.

Having that knowledge gives these stories the sharp-edged quality of something precious preserved under glass. One of my favourite pieces is about taking Sam to a James Bond movie back when Sean

Connery and sexism ruled over the franchise. Sam was an old soul with a quick wit. I'm grateful to have recorded some aspects of his very short life.

Sadness aside, I've had a few chuckles revising the words of a worn-out twenty-something mum. I feel for her, stuck out in the suburbs back when phones were on walls and nobody laughed at a man in a safari suit.

Though a lot has changed since this book was first born, many important things have not. Parents still lie to their kids. Feminism remains a work in progress. And parenting is still the hardest job on Earth.

I hope you enjoy these pieces.

Dear Mum,
I bought a one-way ticket to Homespun Grove.
The streets are paved with nappy wipes.
The neighbours think I have a personality problem because I want
*   to talk to them.*

The kids want me too much.
My husband doesn't want me enough.
Sometimes I forget my name.
Could you lend me the return fare soon?

Love from, Whoeveritwas

HOW IT STARTED

We were all jealous when Linda fell pregnant at fifteen and had to marry her sixteen-year-old boyfriend.

Lucky Linda had snared her man and scored a ticket to adulthood in one hit. We clustered around the desks at the back of the classroom for breathless updates on the pregnancy. Linda had arranged to give birth at exam time, which meant she was excused from study for the whole term. Linda was smart as well as lucky.

When her baby was born (a girl, I think), her husband Darren pretended her hospital bed was a trampoline and jumped up and down on it. Linda complained his antics made her stitches hurt. It sounded *too much* fun.

We all knew boyfriends were a thousand times more fascinating than algebra. Sometimes, I'd gaze around the classroom and wonder who'd be next to fulfil her destiny during a back-seat grapple.

That same year, my sister and I tricked our parents into letting me tag along with her to a party on a British cargo ship. HMV *Huntington* was docked in port to collect butter generously donated by our local dairy cows. After six months at sea, the ship's officers were eager to express their appreciation to the town's womenfolk. My sister persuaded our parents the officers would be gentlemen. Being five years older, she swore to our parents she'd keep an eye on me. I prayed she wouldn't.

The port was transformed at night into a glittering kingdom.

Wind tore at our carefully sprayed hair. The shape of a crane stood out like a giant blackbird against the moon. Our Louis heels caught in the gaps between the sturdy wooden sleepers as we headed towards the ship which was sparkling like an exotic diamond against the wharf. Clutching our visitors passes, we rattled up the gangway.

My sister was right. The officers *were* gentlemen. With their pink and white faces and baby soft hands, they were a different species from the sunburnt farmers who steered us round the Queens Hall on Saturday nights.

Within minutes of entering the dimly lit officers' bar, I fell in lust with the radio officer. An old man of twenty, with the cutest British accent, he reminded me of Paul McCartney. Even though he came from the other side of the world, we had so much in common. His parents had a Golden Retriever called Bracken, which happened to be the name of our street. And his mother liked singing, just like mine. He walked me home, and didn't make stupid comments about the ramshackle Munster house our family inhabited. In fact, he seemed quite impressed.

Aware the clock was ticking – I'd be turning sixteen next March – I turned down the lights and spooned instant coffee into matching mugs. We kissed, and because of Mum's ban on sex before marriage … kissed.

Next morning, I heard the ship's horn moan as it left port. I wrote a poem and knew I was in love. We wrote to each other for three years. His letters had postmarks from romantic places like Panama, Papeete … Bluff. He said maybe one day I could go to England and meet his parents.

The year I turned sixteen, my friend Anna was sent 200 miles away to stay with her aunt for six months. She returned with a sadness in her eyes that wouldn't go away even when she smiled. When I asked what'd happened she just shook her head. I had yet to learn how widespread adoption was back then. Soon after, Anna married a religious guy and asked me to be her bridesmaid. I was sixteen and on the shelf.

Mum's ban on sex before marriage meant I was desperate to tie the knot with someone by the time I was seventeen. To complicate things further, she insisted I must have training for some sort of career before getting hitched.

Flicking through the careers manual in the school library, I never got past the As. Archaeology sounded interesting. So did Architecture, except I wasn't clever enough. I liked the idea of becoming an Artist – but the training course was four years, and I was too desperate to get married to wait that long.

It's funny how the answer to life's great dilemmas is often right under your nose. Mum had worked as a journalist before she was married. Though it was an unusual vocation for a woman at the time, they'd 'let her in' to the newspaper office because so many men were away at World War Two. Even though she'd given up work to become a wife and mother – as any decent woman would in those days – Mum never stopped writing. She kept an arts column on the boil in the local rag through most of her life. I'd grown up with a typewriter hammering in my ears. Anyone could sling a few words together. Better still, the polytech Journalism course in Wellington took only *one year*!

While I was scraping through journalism school with straight C's, there were rumblings of something called Feminism from the university across the town. It seemed to attract well-heeled city girls who never wore homemade clothes. I thought about tearing my bra off and burning it, but that was quite a sacrifice for a 36D. Feminism, I decided, was just a phase, like computers. After finishing the Journalism course, I took a cadetship on Wellington's morning newspaper. It was fun, but my hormones were on fire. I threw the job in and flew to England fresh as our home-grown butter, to stay with my radio officer's parents.

Having spent only two weeks in person with my beloved during the three years we'd been writing letters, I'd moulded him into the myth of the perfect man. Reality had no hope of matching up.

His parents took exception to a big-boned girl from the colonies and threw us out. We married a week later in the Guildford registry office. Only five people were brave enough to turn up for the ceremony. I wore an ankle-length black-and-white dress and sandals in order not to tower over the groom. The celebrant was so bored he forgot to mention the ring. My new husband put it on my finger afterwards outside in the porch. It was raining.

Two weeks later, arranging flowers on top of the toilet cistern in our shabby flat, I realised I'd made a mistake. It was too late. I'd hurt too many people plunging into matrimony at the age of eighteen. Failure wasn't an option.

We headed back to Wellington where he worked on the rail ferries that ploughed between the North and South Islands. After giving birth to Sam at the age of nineteen, I struggled to be the perfect wife and mother. Still restless, unfulfilled, I decided to solve it by having another gorgeous baby boy, Rob, at the age of twenty-one.

After that, I cried a lot. The doctor put me on valium. It made me cry more. Anyone who stood out and made a nuisance of themselves ran the risk of being sent to the 'looney bin' back then. My Uncle Toby had languished behind bars and died in one, mainly because he'd come home from World War One in a state. All of a sudden, the prospect of ending up like that gentle, sensitive man didn't seem so unlikely.

Worried I'd be diagnosed with suburban neurosis (the seventies version of postnatal depression), I threw out the pills and tried to work out who I was.

Stuck between worlds, I was a stay-at-home feminist, a career-minded woman who didn't have a job, a teenage bride masquerading as a grown-up.

In desperation, I turned to the only thing I knew. Sitting at the kitchen table in front of my portable typewriter, I poured out stories about things that made me weep and drove me nuts.

The editor of the local giveaway paper, Brian Kitching, said they made him laugh. He published a few in *The Karori News*.

Soon after, I began writing regular pieces for *The Dominion* (a newspaper people had to pay money for).

And so began decades of column writing.

THE MOTHER'S LIE

It started in the maternity hospital. An ecstatic mother, clutching her stitches, eased herself onto my bed.

'She's done it!' the woman said. 'At last!'

'Who? What?' I asked in a drug-induced haze.

Exasperated by my slowness, she plunged her hands into the pockets of her pink, quilted dressing gown.

'My baby, of course. She just smiled.' I heaved myself onto one elbow and cast aside the James Herriot vet book my husband had brought in. It wasn't doing me any good, anyway. I'd been haunted by dreams of giving birth to twin foals.

'But she's only three hours old,' I said. 'They don't smile till they're at least six weeks.'

'I know. Isn't it wonderful? She's Advanced. Listen? Can you hear her crying? Does that sound like Ancient Greek to you?' When she stood up and left to attend to the needs of her tiny genius, I was relieved. I rolled out of bed and staggered to my bleary-eyed specimen's bassinet. He seemed to have enough problems coping with gravity. Eating, sleeping and filling his pants were his accomplishments.

I picked him up and rested his wobbly, coconut-sized head on my shoulder. 'Go on. Smile, can't you?' I urged. 'Or at least hum a verse of "Moon River".' He didn't seem to hear. I tucked him back in his blanket and waited for the next drug round.

*

Other people's kids slept through the night the minute they left the maternity hospital. They stayed awake most of the day because they were Exceptionally Bright and wanted to absorb what was going on around them. Those kids sat up unaided at six months and spoke about their 'abdomens' at seventeen months.

My kids ate and yelled a lot. I tried not to notice how late it was when they started talking and walking. Then some idiot organisation would ask me to fill in a form about their development. I lied a lot.

Life was difficult for people with Exceptionally Ordinary children.

When a neighbour rang, I sensed the urgency in her voice. 'What class is your boy in this term?' she asked.

'I'm not sure. How can you tell?'

'Was he a Muppet or a Womble last year?'

'How do you mean?'

'His reading group, of course!'

My stomach churned with anxiety. 'I think he was a Muppet.'

'A Muppet?' she gasped.

'Is that not good?'

A significant silence at her end of the phone. 'The Wombles were the top group, you see,' she explained sympathetically.

'Was your Stephanie a Womble?' I spat the words like bullets.

'Yes, as a matter of fact, she was. Are you quite sure he was a Muppet?'

My hand was hot and clammy on the receiver. My breathing fast and shallow. 'He finished the red set of books last year,' I said.

'Oh well,' she sighed. 'That's it.'

'What?'

'Stephanie was halfway into yellow.'

Sweat trickled down my wrists. Should I demand to see the headmaster? 'Do you think he needs a child psychologist?' I asked.

'Oh, no,' she replied soothingly. 'He just isn't Advanced. That's all.'

I wandered round the house, chanting 'my son, the street sweeper'. It didn't have quite the ring of 'my son, the systems analyst'.

He was lying on the floor watching *Mister Ed*. I tripped over him on my way through the living room.

'What's the matter, Mum?'

'I just want you to know I love you no matter what you are. I don't care if you're a Muppet or a Womble!'

'That's okay with me,' he chirped. 'You can be Wonder Woman or Miss Piggy.'

*

Maternity hospitals are great places to learn about contraception. Mothers lounge about in dayrooms like battle-worn soldiers and recount their greatest glories and defeats.

Women love to talk about their guts at the best of times. But there's something in a hospital atmosphere which makes the stories bloodier and more visceral than usual.

'I had an IUD when I got pregnant with this one,' an ashen-faced woman said in a flat voice. 'It just popped out with the baby's head.'

A ruffle of disquiet spread through the room. As if a fowlhouse hen had just laid an egg and the rest were about to try their darnedest to outdo her.

An imposing lady in an expensive dressing gown cleared her throat. 'I was taking the mini-pill,' she announced. 'I didn't forget it once. Still, here I am anyway.'

We replied with respectful silence. It's difficult to assess a person's socio-economic level in hospitals. They're stripped of all the usual embellishments like cars, houses, jobs. All you can go by are the cost and type of dressing gown – an unreliable and unfair method. There are always people who go out and buy a dressing gown specifically designed to intimidate other patients. I don't think I've ever remembered to take a pair of slippers. Besides, everyone's a victim in a maternity hospital. Women are bonded by fear and suspicion of doctors, nurses and modern medicine in general. The ferocity of that sisterhood tends to batter down social barriers.

Still, there was a tone in this woman's voice that suggested she was accustomed to respectful silence. We provided it for a short time.

A girl with skin the colour of shredded coconut looked up from the bootie she was knitting. 'I was using a diaphragm when I got pregnant.' A ruddy-faced mother earth type smiled sadly. 'I studied my mucus and took my temperature for months,' she said. 'Look where it got me.' A woman with haunted eyes claimed her husband had bought the one condom in a hundred the factory man puts a pinprick in to keep the birthrate up.

Mother Earth said she knew someone who'd got pregnant just after her husband had undergone a vasectomy.

The shredded coconut girl sighed. 'Let's face it,' she said. 'The only reliable contraceptive is abstinence.'

The expensive dressing gown started giggling hysterically. Her demented cackle became contagious. It wasn't long before the whole room rocked with nightmarish screeches.

Two nurses, who looked about fourteen years old, put their heads round the door.

'What's the matter with them now?' one said to the other. 'Women who've had babies are insane. Must be the hormones.'

The other, a solid, no-nonsense girl, decided to take charge of the situation. 'Come along now!' she barked in the imperious tone of my old maths teacher. 'It's time you were all downstairs for your lecture.'

'What's today's theme?' I asked.

'We're going to tell you about the advanced types of modern contraceptives that are available,' she clipped. 'Technology is so sophisticated these days, no woman need ever have an unplanned pregnancy.' Rebellion lay heavy in the air. Faces pouted or buried themselves in magazines.

Our fourteen-year-old dictator coughed importantly. 'So you're all coming back next year for another baby, are you?' she threatened.

Magazines were slowly put aside, knitting returned to plastic bags. We shuffled subdued down the shiny corridor behind our two brisk medical superiors.

The two nurses tried to convince us science knew best, but it was hard to take them seriously. They were so young we could've given birth to them. If the condom had burst.

*

I wasn't born a guilty parent. Sometimes I try to cast my mind back to when it first happened.

Was it when I scooped a six-hour-old bundle out of his aquarium-like bassinet at the same time the matron stuck her head round the door?

'You'll spoil that child picking it up all the time!' she snapped.

I tucked the infant back in its box faster than a factory worker packs chocolate chip biscuits.

Or was it when I proudly wheeled my miniature Buddha round a playground he was far too young to appreciate?

An elderly woman jabbed her finger into my belly. 'That baby should have a hat on!' she growled.

I felt devastated by her lack of approval. But it soon became obvious that wherever I pushed a pram I was a target for outspoken opinion. Strangers told me my child was too hot, too cold, underfed, too fat, spoilt, neglected. I believed them all.

Nobody was forthcoming with constructive ideas like babysitting offers.

I stopped going out much.

Then it happened.

Our three-year-old pounded into the house with blood streaming from his left eye. We left the evening meal untouched on the kitchen table, dived into the car and dashed to the nearest medical centre. My foot pressed against the accelerator but still the car wouldn't go fast enough. I clutched the wheel, shaking with anxiety.

Faced with the doctor, I tried to appear light-hearted, humorous. My voice was unworldly. Hysterical.

'I don't know exactly what happened …' Already it sounded as if I was trying to cover up a violent crime. Luckily, the gash wasn't as bad as it seemed. The doctor placed a large white pad over the child's eye.

Hot tears trickled down my face. Perhaps it was relief. Maybe it was a gush of self-pity. The harder I tried to be a perfect parent, the more I seemed to fail.

Then the doctor did a most unmedical thing. He put his arm round my shoulder. 'I know what it's like,' he said. 'I've got kids too. It's terrible when it's your own, isn't it?'

*

There's no doubt about it. Violence is horrible. Love, hate or ignore it, it's part of our make-up, simmering away in our caveman subconscious.

'People are so violent these days it makes me mad. They're so vicious and nasty I want to give them a kick in the pants.'

I nodded in fierce agreement with my friend Sue as our toddlers pummelled each other with plastic blocks.

'I can't stand aggression,' she said. 'How can we expect our kids to grow into peaceful humans when people are such brutes? And if my kid hits your kid one more time I'll clout him!'

'No, no,' I spluttered. 'You're not supposed to hit them. Divert them.'

But the biscuits I shoved at them immediately became new weapons.

'Take that junk food away!' Sue shrieked. 'They'll grow into fatties and nobody will love them.'

'What do you want me to do?'

'Withdraw affection. That's the latest.'

'How can I do that? They're not being lovable in the first place.'

The kids soon tired of the toys they'd broken. Her boy glowered at me. 'Got any guns in this house?'

'No. I don't approve of them.'

'C'mon. Let's go outside.'

They sauntered out the door like a pair of miniature Green Berets.

Sue heaved a sigh. 'I put it down to television. My kids refuse to watch children's programs any more. There's not enough death in *Playschool*. They wait for the news, with the real stuff.'

'Isn't it to do with potty training?' I said, glancing out the window. 'I have a book that says it makes them screwed up and full of loathing.'

Sue didn't seem convinced.

'Isn't that cute?' I said. 'Look at the boys building playhouses out of those old cardboard boxes.'

Sue adjusted her glasses and narrowed her eyes.

'Those are nuclear warheads,' she said.

'Shouldn't they come inside now?' I asked, changing the subject. 'It's so cold they could get bronchitis.'

'But if we call them inside, they might get asthma from the house dust,' Sue said.

If she was passing judgement on my hygiene standards and I had more energy, I might have been tempted to hit her over the head with the nearest frying pan.

Instead, we stared glumly into space.

A CASTLE IN THE GORSE

Nobody tells you. Not when you're a love-sick adolescent. They don't say marriage isn't one long hair-shampoo advertisement.

Nobody tried to enlighten us. The biology teacher droned on about ovum and fruit flies. We knew there was more to it than that. Deep down we knew we had just met (or were about to) the Love of our Life. It was to do with pop songs and dancing too close and clammy hands in the cinema's back row. We knew this was It.

Something made us believe we weren't the ones who'd end up in a suburban dead-end street. Our spotty boyfriends would carry us off to lives of endless bliss and mutual devotion. It wasn't all that important if the babies came now or later.

Well, I guess the girls would say I've made it. I've got my man and kids (in the respectable order). But the castles in the air were already occupied. We've had to settle for suburbia.

Gorse glows yellow most of the year in the vacant land blocks that surround us. The current housing slump ensures we'll be seeing yellow for a good few seasons yet.

We live in frontier land. It's nothing like as glamorous as the one Walt Disney created. Our 'charming, mock-colonial 4-br, lge. lounge, 1-wc investment home' is perched on the edge of an artificially created clay mountain. Whoever thought of dumping truckloads of soil over a once picturesque valley to create a new subdivision must've regarded himself as a minor deity.

The northerly wind belts down the road most days, but sometimes the landscape can be beautiful in an Andrew Wyeth way. Not that I can remember Wyeth including gorse in his bleak American landscapes.

We moved here four years ago in hope new houses would sprout either side of us and spread down the hill. It never happened. We tell our friends how great it is to have all these wide open spaces. Our two boys think they're growing up on a farm.

I never thought we'd wind up in a place like this. Let me tell you how we got here. Our first house was up 103 steps. The view was beautiful, but dragging a baby and his paraphernalia up those steps several times a day was not.

'Why not sell?' a clever person said. 'We're on to our fourth house. Our next home will be really something.'

Her subtle use of language wasn't lost on me. Though she was currently living in a house right now, she'd soon be moving up to a 'home'. We were definitely still in a 'house'.

The concept was new to me. You spend your life buying houses, each slightly bigger and better than the last. Once you've reached the mansion stage, you snap up a four-hectare lifestyle block in the back of nowhere. You buy jodhpurs, a spinning wheel and, hey hey, you're top of the real estate dung heap – providing you prefer black sheep to people.

Things weren't working out like that for us. Our modest mound of money hadn't grown any bigger. Every move we made, we just had to borrow more. We were hopeless amateurs.

We sold the steps and moved to a charming little house. Did I say little? Baby number two announced his imminent arrival; there was no bedroom for him. My nerves weren't strong enough to cope with putting two infants in the same room. Determined to be practical, we decided to leave that friendly neighbourhood. We sifted through real estate ads and opted for the ultimate in functionalism. There were no holes in the roof, no steps, no rotting wood in the basement.

I was willing to overlook the questionable architecture on the street winding up to our house. Every ancient civilisation – from Egypt to Tudor England – was replicated in chipboard and paint.

The depressing talk about new subdivisions was based on intangibles, I thought. What did it matter if you had to drive two miles to the shops? In a few years the place would be lush with vegetation and echoing with the happy cries of children. Since then I've been educated.

The emptiness of our subdivision has a strange effect on our sparsely scattered neighbours. A few have knuckled down and acquired a Wild West camaraderie. Others seem to be having breakdowns.

After all, it's a challenge to imagine yourself as exiled royalty in your neo-Georgian manor when there are no servants and no adoring peasants to bow at your gate. There's a desolate air about the neo-Georgians as they lock up their double garages in the evenings.

Wives stay shrouded behind net curtains, like Grimm's fairy-tale princesses. They watch *The Young and the Restless*, gulp a few valiums and wait for hubby to stumble up the elegantly curved concrete steps after a hard day's accounting.

There's no set pattern of behaviour in this harsh emptiness. Hearty friendliness is not the Thing. In fact, this neighbourhood could teach the inhabitants of Calcutta a thing or two about caste systems.

Around here, there are town-house people and proper-house people. It's vital to stick to your own level of square footage. Proper-house people wouldn't dream of inviting town-house people over for drinks, for instance, unless they were some kind of trendy socialists.

One man walks his large black poodle past our house at precisely 8.45 a.m. every day. He ignores the greetings I hurl in his direction. Nevertheless he's become part of my life. His punctuality is reassuring. It reminds me it's time to change the nappy bucket solution.

One day 8.45 came, but no man with poodle. Eight-fifty and still no sign. I felt restless.

Nine-fifteen. At last, two striding figures appeared in the distance and swooped past the gate.

'You're late!' I called, out of relief more than anything else.

I might as well have thrown a brick at him. He put his head down and ran.

I still wonder what I did wrong. Perhaps he thought I was making advances. At least I know where I stand now as we determinedly ignore each other every morning.

Subdivision living is a strange mixture of rural isolation and urban cut-throat.

Weekends see car-loads of house addicts cruising menacingly around the curves of our new streets. Their curiosity is transparent. They nudge up our driveway, wind down their windows and stare. Sometimes I wave from the front room. They don't respond. To them I'm just a plastic mannequin in a shop window.

Further down the hill, a freshly arrived neighbour was alarmed to encounter one of these property snoops with his face pressed against her bedroom window.

'Sorry,' he said. 'I didn't think this house was finished.'

*

Everyone knows about suburban neurosis. It happens to all of us. Except me. I never worry. It's a pointless waste of energy.

I thought I was going to worry the other day. The house was falling down. Well, not actually falling down. Disintegrating. I found this chewed-out, rotten-looking hole in the bathroom floor and felt a wave of what might've been worry coming on.

I phoned the builder. 'Remember me?' I said. 'You built this house four years ago and it's falling apart already.'

'You're the hacienda on Bonanza Avenue?'

'No. The mock-pioneer on Homespun Grove.'

'Don't know what you're complaining about. I put your house together with genuine staples.'

'It's just this hole in the floor.'

'Chipboard, you mean.'

'Looks more like oatmeal.'

'Ah yes. Ventilation.'

'But it only appeared today.'

An irritated sigh rattled through the phone. 'Don't you think I knew you'd need air through that bathroom some day?'

'What about this weatherboard that's swelling and cracking, windows that won't shut, and the way the roof seems to be edging off the house?'

'People'll pay millions for properly ventilated houses like yours in a few years,' he said.

'So there's nothing to worry about?'

'Just let me get on with my art,' he said.

I put the phone down and decided there are lots of things not to worry about. Like when:

- our three-year-old son wears mascara and says he wants big breasts and pantyhose when he grows up. 'He wants a beard too,' my husband added. Oh well. There's always been a leaning that way in our family

- I think of all the times I've said the wrong thing to people. How their faces changed shape as the message sank in. How things might've been if I hadn't said it

- the bank manager recognises me in the supermarket – and changes aisles

- chocolate on biscuits seems thinner and there's indecipherable language on the apple juice can

- I wonder if the milkman accepts Visa cards

- what the mole doctor said was nothing takes on a green tinge and is definitely bigger than yesterday. Come to think of it, she said 'Nothing' with exaggerated nonchalance and half turned away when she said it

- I climb on the bus and teenagers lower their voices and giggle in a malevolent way

- neighbours' disposable nappies blow out of their rubbish tin onto our lawn
- the rag I've used to wash dog shit out of the carpet flies down the hill to settle on a mock-Georgian's camellia bush
- Six-year-old says he'll die if he doesn't get a $90 robot for his birthday
- people stare into my face as if they're noticing my eyes look in slightly different directions. When I was a kid, a surgeon had two goes at straightening my squint. He must've suffered from terminal clumsiness.

I went back to the bathroom and had another look at that hole in the floor. A masterpiece, really. The cracks in the ceiling and warped weatherboards are proof that that builder's ahead of his time.

*

Some people think a woman's love life becomes monotonous once she's married and producing children.

Not true. My own workaday activities in the depths of suburbia have their high points. I'm not ashamed to talk about them.

Take the postie, for instance. I suppose I shouldn't mention him in case he takes fright and asks for his round to be changed. Still, I'll risk it.

It's worth staying in till 10.30 or 11 a.m. just for the sight of those hairy brown muscular legs striding past the front gate. Even the dullest brown envelope has a hint of glamour about it. I know it has been jostled about in the canvas bag of this bronzed god.

Sometimes we exchange pleasantries which reek with innuendo.

'Nice day,' I say.

'Might be going to rain later,' he says, slapping the latest bill in my sweaty palm. I watch him continue his jaunt down the hill. His mind is probably absorbed with theories about health food or Farrah Fawcett.

My day is a little flat if he's off and someone else does his round.

But don't think I've put all my eggs in one basket with this postie. There are other men.

The dustman's chunky limbs are second-glance material. I have to be up early to catch a glimpse of him – but I'm usually too busy trying to stop the dog reducing him to pet jelly to be able to relax and enjoy myself.

If I'm in the mood for something along the lines of a Latin lover, I go to the fish-and-chip shop. 'Yes?' he says, wiping smooth hands on his oil-spattered apron.

I stare into his hooded black eyes. A face like that should be writing symphonies. 'Five fish-and-chips,' I breathe.

His long delicate fingers place baskets of battered fish in oil. Already he is serving someone else, but I know he hasn't forgotten my order.

Sometimes I think of something clever to say and his eyes flash. Usually I can't.

He drains the chips and douses them in salt. 'Two-a-dollars sixty,' he says in that husky voice.

I fumble for three dollars and drop some coins on the floor. He smiles because he knows my mind is on something else.

The hairdresser's is not a happy hunting ground. The gentleman there is more interested in my husband. Mind you, plenty of little old ladies leave that shop with radiant faces. I guess it's okay if you're into Oedipus.

I head for the bank. The teller pretends he is immaculate and polite to the core of his three-piece suit. 'How would you like it?' he asks without daring to look me in the eye.

I take a deep breath. 'Three tens and a five, please.'

There are casual encounters like the telephone repair man, who oozed Irish charm down the receiver. 'Has the static completely gone now, Mrs Brown?'

I felt a jolt under my ribs. 'Yes, I think so.'

Sometimes, I think all this is unhealthy and I send away for night-class brochures. People always suggest night classes to solve any housebound woman's problem, ranging from exhaustion to unwanted pregnancy. Back home they'd say 'Have another baby' – which doesn't help either predicament.

I even rang a neighbour to see if she thought I was in need of therapy.

'I'd love to talk,' she said. 'But it's getting on for 10.30 and the postie's due. Have you seen the legs on that man?'

BUT WHAT DO YOU *REALLY* DO?

Some day in your life you have to make a momentous decision. Will you send your kid to playgroup or kindergarten?

It mightn't be the sort of problem that would have kept JFK awake during the Cuban Missile Crisis, but it's serious.

Kindergarten people shudder to think what goes on in playgroup homes. The kids never have haircuts and run barefoot most of the time. I've even heard whispers about half-baked theories on herbal vaccinations.

You can pick a playgroup kid a mile off. On the bus, it's the four-year-old tugging at the buttons on his mother's shirt and demanding to be breast fed.

A playgroup mother is instantly recognisable by the black rings under her eyes. This is because she's been on too many Duties.

A Duty has nothing to do with British taxes and the Boston Tea Party. It's three hours of hell spent swimming in a sea of screaming three-year-olds. A Duty mother has to pretend to get significant rewards from scraping stomach-churning lumps of dough from the soles of her shoes. That she adores stopping Jeremy murdering Simon with a hammer. And yes, she'd LOVE to sign up for the parent-helper course so she can do it with Greater Awareness and more often.

The only way to get out of Duties is to have a baby. I know one mum who arranged to get pregnant every year so she wouldn't have to do a Duty.

Another friend said she hated Duties because she was always sent outside in miserable weather to look after the hardy brats who played out there hail or snowstorm. 'I could swear all the other mothers are inside talking about me,' she said.

True, playgroup mothers can be extremely cliquey. They seem to share everything, including husbands (who are usually psychologists).

But the biases run both ways. Playgroup people think all kindy mothers wear tailored trouser suits and go to Tupperware parties.

Kindy fathers are nearly always right-wing accountants.

The only reason I sent my kid to playgroup was because he could start there a year earlier than he could at kindergarten. I was so desperate to get him out of the house a few hours a week I was prepared to do anything – even Duties.

One Duty day, I lifted my head from a tangled knot of children and saw a mother staring across the playing field at a neat white building.

'What's that?' I asked.

'The kindergarten,' she said sternly. 'It's a dumping ground.'

'You mean you can actually dump your kid there – no Duties, no nothing?'

She looked at me with disdain. 'Yes – if you're That Sort of Parent.'

I quickly agreed that dumping was a terrible thing.

For several nights I had blissful dreams about dumping grounds. I saw myself waving to my kid's happy face as I teetered out the kindergarten gate in my kindy mother's uniform – a vinyl coat and shiny high-heeled boots.

I caught myself smiling slyly over the next few days. I was going to beat the system.

I hadn't told anyone at playgroup, but we had our names on the *kindergarten waiting list*!

Then I realised the move would be social suicide. Playgroup parents would hate me because I'd shown myself up as a dumper.

It'd take years to convince kindy mothers I wasn't merely a spy from across the playing field.

When the kindy teacher rang to tell me my kid could start my heart leapt to my throat. I wanted to say yes so badly, but in the end I had to confess we were playgroup people. She dropped the receiver as if it was molten lava.

I later found out that that dumping ground stuff is just somebody's wishful fantasy. Playgroup and kindy have one thing in common: the second you set foot in the door someone swoops and begs you to be president, secretary or treasurer.

My friend Sue got roped into the kindergarten president's chair on her first day.

'I can't understand,' I said. 'Here you are, president of the dumping ground, and you spend all week going to meetings and answering a red-hot phone.'

'Hang on.' She snatched up her phone like an overworked businessman. 'Two thousand dollars for a sandpit? Is that how much it costs to build a sandpit these days? … Okay we'll negotiate. Next Wednesday 2.30? Fine.'

'You kindy guys have it easy,' I continued. 'You don't have to do Duties.'

Sue slammed the phone down and turned crimson.

'Duties?' she said. 'Of course we do Duties! They're part of our parent involvement scheme.' I wonder if a creche is any less work.

*

Having a thwarted opera star for a mother wasn't always easy. She often made us feel she was slumming it looking after Dad and us kids. It was as if our existence was stifling the life of an exotic flower that belonged in a global hothouse. I felt guilty and had no idea how to help her, apart from growing up and leaving home as soon as possible.

Mum always kept 'a little job' going, just for pin money, she explained. Becoming an untrained kindergarten assistant seemed a desperate choice for someone who didn't particularly like children, but she did it for a few years. I now understand it didn't matter what sort of work it was. She needed a job to give herself an identity beyond wife and motherhood. It gave her an excuse to buy a car, an ancient Austin with a crank handle.

When someone from the local paper phoned to ask her to write a weekly arts page, her excitement bounced off the kitchen walls. She didn't think twice about resigning from the kindergarten. The typewriter would emit regular thuds, like heartbeats, as her two fingers pounded reviews and feature articles onto rectangular pieces of copy paper. With her spectacles sliding down her nose as she bent over the machine, she was consumed, the closest I saw her to content.

I was proud of her for refusing to be a 'normal' stay-at-home mum. Most of my friends had fathers who said no wife of theirs was ever going to get a job.

Back then women were expected to content themselves with afternoon tea parties, serving scones from tea trollies in the safety of their own living rooms. The most common conversation starter was 'What does your husband do?'

The assumption was they were too busy changing nappies and firing the furnace of their husbands' careers to be worth talking about.

Even more disturbing was 'What did you do before you were married?' It implied life stopped the minute a woman plunged a knife into a wedding cake.

All that's changed since women's lib and the pill came along. Still, when a stranger gets that earnest look I know the question will be equally squirm-inducing.

'What do you do?' they say.

A friend replied that she was trying to bring up five kids. 'Yes, but what do you *really* do?' the questioner persisted. 'You seem an intelligent woman. You must be doing something besides baby farming?'

Women with kids are supposed to be finishing PhDs, exploring the highlands of New Guinea and writing sex manuals during some elusive thing called Spare Time.

Child-raising can be frustrating, exhausting and, let's be honest here, boring. The fascination of childish conversation can reach its limits. There've been times when I've felt if I had to struggle out of bed in the middle of the night to fetch a fifteenth glass of water for a demanding small person I'd collapse into a heap of blancmange.

There are also the good times that are idealised on TV advertisements. But ecstatic, slow motion romps along the beach can be short-lived if the family is under financial or other pressure and mum is depressed and lonely.

The reality of motherhood makes for dreary social chitchat. So women sit around and say to each other, 'What do you do?'

I've spent ages listening to and admiring the long lists of other mothers' extramural activities. Mousey ladies go to encounter groups; others pour water up their noses and other orifices at yoga classes. Hypochondriacs learn acupuncture and matriarchs teach Latin part time – for mental stimulation rather than financial gain.

All this talk made me feel inferior and dull. Had the automatic washing machine made that much difference to motherhood? If so, I was behind the times.

Then I met a friend who had just finished several years' playgroup supervising.

'Well,' I said. 'What are you going to do now you're going to have more spare time?'

'Nothing,' she said.

'What?' I gasped. 'Surely you'll go to university or start singing in a pub or something?'

'Nope.'

'But what about our friends? They're all out doing big things.'

She looked at me, incredulous. 'You don't believe all that crap, do you?' she said. 'They make it up.'

*

I don't know any parents who don't try their best. It's just that some people's best can be damned infuriating. Especially at Christmas. I was minding my own business at the toy shop when a denim-clad woman pushed past me to assail the assistant.

'Have you got any toy trucks or guns?' she asked.

The assistant pointed her at the boys' section.

'I'm not shopping for *boys*!' said the affronted customer. 'We want our two little girls to grow up without gender bias.'

I smothered a wry smile and battled on with my own sexist Christmas shopping. My husband will have to survive without a shoulder bag this year. Aunt Lila would be astonished if I gave her a toolkit.

A non-sexist Christmas seemed a luxury. With a mortgage longer than our telephone number, my thoughts were focused on how we could afford Christmas at all.

I climbed back in the car and dived for a fifty-cent coin wedged in the passenger seat only to find it was a piece of tin foil from a fake Christmas tree.

But Christmas shoppers weren't the only ones going out of their way to be politically correct. By some bizarre combination of circumstances I'd just been elected president of playgroup. I don't know how it happened. I must've been out to it on valium at the time. President sounds flash, but it just meant I was too dumb to be treasurer and not reliable enough to be secretary.

I wasn't sure what presidents did, apart from arranging the end-of-year pageant. It was just to give the kids an excuse to dress up and run around on stage. But things were turning out more complicated than I'd imagined. The phone was running faster than a debutante with diarrhea.

'Hello? You're organising the end-of-year performance, aren't you?'

She didn't give me time to answer.

'I heard we're doing *Hansel and Gretel*. I'm disgusted.'

'Oh?'

'It's a nasty, sexist, violent story. A terrible thing to expose children to.'

'Really? We could arrange a bit of role-swapping and cut back on the tomato sauce?'

'I don't see how,' she said. 'Hansel's the adventurous boy who takes them out to get lost. The witch puts him in a cage while Gretel does the housework! It's not healthy having those people pushed into ovens all over the place, either.'

'How about *Cinderella*?' I asked.

'No way! It presents marriage as the ideal for every girl.'

'*The Three Bears*?'

'Helpless woman syndrome again,' she snapped.

'*Jack and the Beanstalk*?'

'An obsession with phallic symbols.'

'How about a nice Christmas nativity?'

'We can't shove religion down their throats!'

'Maybe we should give up on the idea,' I sighed.

'As a matter of fact, I've just bought a fascinating preschool encyclopedia. I could read a chapter or two. Let me see, here's something they'd like – "The Origin of Sperm".'

'Fine, fine.'

'Good. Then all we need is someone to be Mother Christmas.'

I could feel the sun setting over my stint as playgroup president.

*

I wish to God my kids had sat in on that reading. It might've solved a few problems later.

The realities of life hit like a cattle truck when he turned six. 'Life used to be so sweet when I was five,' he sighed on the beach one day. 'It's all sour now.' I had been going out of my way to make life positively syrupy for him at the time. I'd been charging over rocks like an advertisement mother, throwing sticks for the dog and pointing out fascinating phenomena like detergent bubbles on the shore.

I'd been unaware of this disillusioned old man of six glaring moodily at the waves.

A few days later I did a double-take when I found him mesmerised by something in the wardrobe. He wore the expression bit-part actors try to imitate when they play primitive natives meeting white men for the first time. It's not often you see the look of sheer wonderment on the face of a six-year-old – unless he's watching television.

I peered around the wardrobe door to see what the source of interest was. It appeared to be my husband's trousers.

He stared at them with respect and awe.

'What is it?' I asked.

'I came out of Dad's jeans, you know,' he replied softly, as if it wasn't done to speak too loudly in front of them.

I realised with a sinking feeling I'd failed in yet another area of parenting. 'I think you mean the other sort,' I said. 'You can't buy G-E-N-E-S in a department store.'

He looked at me with an aloof expression as I embarked on a garbled, scientific explanation which left us both confused.

You're not allowed to talk about storks any more and you're not allowed to blush and say, 'Wait till you're older.'

Remember when you were a kid and your mother took you to visit little old ladies who'd produce a copy of *Snow White* for you to read while they talked? Nowadays they give kids *Where Did I Come From?* to peruse while you're sipping tea.

My friends beam delightedly when their preschoolers disappear into bedrooms to play Gynaecology (it's not called Doctors and Nurses any more). I'm embarrassed to say my kids play with trucks. I sometimes catch a mother smiling charitably at them.

'Why don't you run along and play Gynaecology with the others?' I say quickly.

'Brrrrrrmmmm!'

Other people's kids know enough to write an updated edition of *The Hite Report*. Mine play with Lego.

When people started to imply my kids were repressed I tried not to worry. Then one day, I let it slip out casually: 'You do know where babies come from, don't you?'

'Yeah, sure!'

'Oh good.' (Phew!)

'When a woman wants a baby she swallows one and puts it in her tummy.'I patted him on the head and rushed to the nearest kinky bookshop for kids. It was all there: *Reproduction can be Fun, Nine Months is Long Enough, Mummy has an Abortion.* I grabbed a selection and embarked on making my kids as accomplished at playground obstetrics as anyone else's.

We worked through heavily illustrated pages. One book used cartoon characters with evil grins to get the idea across – what an artistic challenge to draw cartoon genitals. It made the whole thing smutty. Another indulged in obscure symbolism – white horses, crashing waves.

After several evenings, I felt I'd done my best. I scanned the kids' faces for knowing expressions. They seemed to be there.

Our six-year-old slammed the last book shut, his face hazy with thought.

'Could you put those old jeans of Dad's away for me somewhere, Mum? I might need them when I grow up.'

WE ALL KNOW SOMEONE WHO KNOWS SOMEONE ...

It had been a perfect dinner – well, almost. The host and hostess were almost as young and beautiful as the other couple they'd invited. I guess we'd been asked along to fill in the gaps.

Sipping our coffee, we drank in the hand-made patchwork curtains and the lingering aroma of incense.

Conversation was witty and could have been mistaken for sophisticated. It would have been elegant, had the host's grandmother not insisted on staying the weekend.

He seemed pleased to have her at first. After all, the extended family is so Now. But she slurped her soup and didn't get the gist of their political patter. She was deaf most of the time, so it was simpler to ignore her.

The other couple had just produced a baby. They were unmarried, of course. 'We just couldn't see the point of signing a piece of paper,' she said. 'We're happy the way we are. The nurses called me Mrs Taylor. What a laugh! I'd always say, "No, nurse. Miss".'

It seemed delightful. They adored each other. Then the reality of their oh-so-modern lifestyle slowly unwound.

'The baby's got my name, of course,' the father said. 'When people ask me who Irene is, I don't bother with that "my lover" nonsense. I say she's the cook!'

He leant back in his chair, pink with satisfaction. Irene looked a little pale and uncomfortable.

'But surely there must be some differences from ordinary marriage?' I asked. 'For example, are you monogamous?'

'Shhh!' hissed the host. 'For God's sake! You'll shock Granny!'

We all darted an anxious look at Granny. She seemed to be dozing in her chair, thank goodness.

'Well, are you?' I whispered.

'Of course we are!' the young father snapped. 'Shhh!'

The host and his wife tittered. 'That's extraordinary,' the hostess whispered. 'We had a church wedding five years ago. Wrote our own service and cut out any reference to monogamy. Sounds too much like monotony.'

'Yes,' the host said as he eyed the women at the table enthusiastically. 'Ours is an open marriage.'

Granny snorted in her sleep. We all jumped, but she dreamed off again.

'The definition of fidelity really is a problem for today's couples,' the host continued as he toyed earnestly with his coffee spoon.

His wife ladled generous quantities of sugar into my husband's cup. 'There are so many more choices open to people now,' she said.

One of Granny's eyes rolled open. The topic quickly changed. But Granny had something to say. 'You needn't think I haven't heard what you've been rambling on about.'

'More tea, Granny?' 'Get me a whiskey,' she croaked.

Her grandson obliged.

'You think you're on to something new?' Gran said, watching the liquid curl into her glass. 'One of your granddad's friends asked me to sleep with him once.'

Our young mouths dropped open.

'What did you do, Gran?' our chastened host asked.

Gran jutted her chin in a defiant sort of way as we waited in pregnant silence.

'What's one slice out of a cut loaf?' she said.

*

To think I looked forward to becoming an adult when I was a kid. I couldn't wait to be thoroughly grown-up about everything. There is something, however, people never grow up about.

Everyone knows someone who knows someone who does it. But does anyone know anyone who actually does it? More to the point, does anyone do it? Wife swapping, that is.

If the party's getting boring and Bruce has gone on for too long about the delights of Marxist theory, there's one way to shut him up …

'I know someone who knows someone who does it.' He'll get an unworldly gleam in his eye.

'Really? We used to know a couple who did it, but they've moved out of town.'

Already people were drawn to our conversation like sparrows to bread on a winter lawn. A lady with spectacles and a long nose directed a snaky grin at nobody in particular. 'We had friends who went to key parties. They'd throw everyone's house keys into the middle of the room then the men would shut their eyes and choose a key. Harry and Lucinda gave it up after a while. Harry kept choosing his own house key. Said it was infuriating.'

A trim woman with too much green eyeshadow and lambskin boots twisted her foot on the carpet. 'Sounds damn sexist to me. Why don't they call them husband-swapping parties?'

'The men wouldn't dream of being objectified like that,' the spectacles said. 'They'd feel threatened. Besides, it must be difficult enough as it is for them to arrange so many repeat performances.'

'We used to know some people,' Bruce said. 'He was the one who started it. Put the ad in *Forum* and all that. But his wife got much more fun out of it. He became exhausted and wanted to give it up. She wouldn't let him.'

A thoughtful silence.

'I don't suppose I'd mind if my husband wanted to do it,' the lambskin boots said slowly. 'Heaven knows he could do with the exercise.'

'But how would you find a couple you both liked in that sort of way?' the spectacles chipped in.

I shuffled a selection of couples through my mind. Had I deliberately chosen women friends whose husbands were unattractive?

My own experiences as a swinger were limited to the day our local politician knocked on the door.

'Who are you going to vote for?' he asked.

'I don't know yet,' I said. 'I play elections by ear.'

He licked his pencil. 'I'll put you down as a swinger then.'

'I'd rather you didn't. What do you mean anyway?'

'Swinging voter,' he chanted as if he'd spoken to one stupid housewife too many that morning.

Back at the dinner party, Bruce cleared his throat. 'I hear it's terribly formal,' he said. 'You're not allowed to talk to each other after you've, you know, done it.'

'Sounds rather impersonal ...'

'Probably more fun than going to sleep in front of the television,' the boots added enthusiastically.

Personally, at that moment I could think of nothing more sensually arousing than the thought of dozing off on the sofa.

'What sort of people actually do it?' I asked.

'Oh everyone,' Bruce said, taking on the role of expert, as he liked to do on most subjects.

Bother. There I was again. Missing out on something everyone else is doing.

'When did you last go to one?' I asked respectfully.

'What *me*?' Bruce replied. 'Go to a swingers' party? You must be joking!'

He fluffed out his homespun jersey like a startled rooster, then settled. 'No, everyone goes to them. *Except* us.'

The long-nosed lady's spectacles had nearly fallen off with excitement. 'There must be hundreds of those sorts of parties going on in this suburb this very weekend,' she said.

I looked over her shoulder out the window. Cosy yellow house lights beamed benignly from across the road.

'Surely not?'

'This suburb's notorious for it,' the boots said.

Bruce added he thought it happened mainly in small towns where there was nothing better to do.

I thought I'd rather go back to listening to him banging on about the joys of socialism after all. But the topic had caused quite a bit of interest. I left them to it, grinding their feet into the shag-pile.

Our neighbour Maude had caught my eye. She was sitting alone in the corner looking left out.

Poor Maude's a conventional person. Backbone of society. No one would dare say anything to her that wasn't church fairs or knitting patterns.

But this night – perhaps it was the wine – I decided to shock her.

I strode across the room.

'I know someone who knows someone who does it,' I said with a mischievous grin.

'Not that again.' She rolled her eyes and swiped an imaginary fly in the air. 'I gave that up years ago.'

*

I haven't been to a wedding in years. All our friends are either single, live together or got married before it went out of fashion. A fair number of the latter are getting divorced, keeping lawyers in Porsches.

Lately, society has done one of its weird flashback twists, and weddings are all the rage again. When an invitation arrived in the mail, I examined it to make sure it wasn't a joke. It wasn't. Turning the card in my hand, I experienced the chill of a brand new phobia – wedding present anxiety.

My mother always gave every bride and groom she knew a crystal bowl. At each wedding reception, Mum's crystal bowl would be put on display on the gift table, alongside the fifteen other identical bowls the couple had received.

Wedding presents leave no room for fun or originality, though believe me I've tried. My sister and her husband never really liked the concrete gnome I gave them. He crouches under a hedge in her back garden like a private detective. I imagine her children have become fond of him.

But what to give today's modern couple – a novelty vibrator? It would be humiliating to receive a note asking if they could exchange it because they have three already.

Our own wedding was celebrated with a plague of towels. I would have danced naked at the registry office for a pair of sheets or even a small crystal bowl. My fingers would eagerly rip open the ding-dong-bell paper.

'How lovely! Towels ! So ... useful!'

There must have been some sinister psychological link. Why did people associate us with towels? Was it because we were too young to be getting married? People at that time associated youth with uncleanliness.

Or were we so petulant and insufferable they thought towels were the only thing that wouldn't cause offence?

This new batch of marriages will be a different tube of confetti from anything we fumbled our way into. Women will have learnt from our mistakes. They'll be liberated and assertive from the start. Instead of spiralling into insanity off the edge of a cliff in outer suburbia, they'll balance dazzling careers with wonderful marriages and fulfilling family lives.

Now where can I get my hands on a crystal bowl?

MARRIAGE – WHOSE IDEA WAS IT ANYWAY?

If you've got a revolting habit, your husband knows about it in 3D and Technicolor.

And when do you ever see him at his best? Perhaps it's when he's rosy with alcohol at the Things' party. There he is, backing Mrs Thing into a corner with a story which was funny when you first heard it five years ago.

Mrs Thing laughs because Mr Thing has an even more boring story he repeats whenever he gets the chance.

I think my husband was lucky, though. He married someone with no bad habits. Not only that, I'm incredibly tolerant.

At least, I thought I was.

I'm not sure when it began. It can't have been long ago. My husband started making small, explosive popping noises with his lips. Not all the time – or even very often. They weren't loud. Sometimes they sounded more like a hiss than a pop.

That's okay, I thought in my usual benevolent mood. I just happened to marry a lip popper.

He lay on the sofa reading the newspaper – and popping his lips.

'What are you doing that for?' I asked kindly.

'I like to keep up with current events,' he replied.

'No. I mean popping your lips like that.'

'Like what?'

'Pop! Like that.'

'I don't do that, do I?' (Pop!)

'You did it just then!'

He seemed genuinely surprised. I'd made my point. It was just a matter of time. He'd give it up.

He didn't. The popping developed a regular pattern. He used pops as punctuation marks at the end of important sentences. He popped at the dinner table and then at breakfast. Stranger still, he popped when he collapsed into bed every night.

Our friends Dave and Sue came for a meal one night. He never popped when we had company. It wasn't long before I noticed Dave drumming his fingers on the table. He spoke normally, looked reasonably comfortable. Why then, the constant drumming?

Perhaps he wished he was home in front of the television or maybe he was allergic to our food. Or was it me?

It was as if the frantic tapping fingers lived totally apart from his amiable face. The drum roll reached a crescendo. It drowned all conversation. Enormous fingers hammering on wood were all I could see and hear.

'Dave, stop that!' I yelled.

His fingers shot under the table as if they'd been scorched. An uncomfortable silence. I tingled with embarrassment.

'Sorry, I didn't –'

'No, no,' Sue interrupted. 'I'm glad you told him. He's always doing it at home.'

'Yes,' Dave said. 'And Sue picks her nose when she watches television. Drives me mad.'

She shot him a glower to melt igloos. He pretended not to see it.

'When I was a schoolkid I used to have a friend who was a champion shoplifter. I gave up being his lookout; it got too dangerous. A few seconds before he stole anything he'd be overcome with nervous sneezing. The whole shop would be staring at him by the time he got near something. Everyone has bad habits,' Dave said.

'Yes, everyone,' I said, to make him feel comfortable.

Everyone?

After they'd gone I stared soulfully at the streetlights from the kitchen window. Surely the world was divided into those who had bad habits and those who put up with them?

'I don't have any bad habits, do I?' I asked my husband.

He popped significantly. 'Only the way you sniff absolutely everything before you put it in the washing machine. Or strew clothes over the entire bedroom, talk loudly about sex at family gatherings –'

'Stop!'

I didn't notice the popping so much after that. In fact, I can't recall if he gave it up or not.

*

When I think things are really going wrong, I remember the Smiths. It makes me feel much better.

Dinner at the Smiths always ends in an argument. I don't know why we keep going there, really. It's just that we asked them once, and they asked us back, then we … you know how it is.

Besides, they seem to enjoy having an audience to fight in front of. We don't mind watching either. It makes our discussions back home about who left the ring around the bath seem like chickenfeed.

They fight about anything – death, sex, politics. But the battle that still stands out in my mind is one about something far less grand.

It had been a pleasant enough evening. The score at coffee time was about four/four. Meg had triumphed on the Jehovah's Witness issue.

'The only way to get rid of them is to be rude,' she said in that defiant tone of hers.

'I don't agree,' husband Collin snapped. 'There was one on the doorstep this very afternoon. I was extremely polite and he went away quite happily.'

I noticed distant tapping.

'Do you get opossums on your roof?' I asked.

'No, it's the door,' Meg said. 'I'll get it.'

She scuttled into the hall and returned, glowering at Collin. 'It's two gentlemen for you, dear. One says he was here this afternoon and there are a few aspects of Armageddon he and his friend would like to clarify.'

It took a while for things to settle down after that. He said the wine tasted like the cheap stuff his sister had left behind last week. Meg said no. She had bought it yesterday and it was quite expensive.

They charged out to the kitchen to compare labels. The two bottles were the same price and brand. Stalemate.

Collin gained ground as time progressed. He knew the rate of inflation in Iran. The evening was drawing to a typically turbulent close. My husband yawned and mentioned how our babysitter was charging enough to buy her own shopping centre.

I stood up and thanked them for a lovely evening. My husband nodded and reached for his jacket.

'Whose turn is it tonight?' Collin asked drowsily.

A cloud of tension settled over the room.

'Yours!' Meg said.

'I did them last night,' he said, his eyes bright and unblinking, like a lizard's.

'No you didn't.'

'*We*'ll do them,' I said brightly. 'We *love* doing dishes, don't we?'

My husband agreed, adding we especially liked scrubbing other people's pots and pans.

'We never let guests do the dishes,' Meg snapped.

My husband suggested they could leave them till the morning.

'And face that revolting sight over my sunflower seed muesli?' Collin sniffed. 'You're joking.'

We felt like caterpillars in poppies at Flanders before the battle – about to be trampled by a war that had nothing to do with us.

'Well, I'm not doing them,' Meg snarled as she turned her cup in her hand like a weapon. 'I'm sick of dishes. It's always my turn!'

Collin's mouth became a line. His neck went the colour of a rooster's comb.

'I hate washing those plates!' he yelled. 'Plates always win in the end. That willow pattern will still be there when I'm dead and gone.'

My husband held up my coat so I could fumble into the armholes. We backed out the door and hurried down their path. Tinkling sounds from inside suggested Meg and Collin would outlive at least part of their dinner set.

We didn't see them for a while. But a few months later Meg rang again.

'Do come round,' she said.

I hesitated.

'Don't worry, we've got a dishwasher now.'

It was a pleasant enough evening. Meg and Collin weren't getting on badly. I was talking about returning to our babysitter, who needed fifteen hours' sleep, when I noticed Collin was on edge. He was giving Meg the old lizard eyes. She acknowledged his silent challenge.

'Whose turn is it?' she snapped.

'But I thought you didn't have this problem any more,' I said. 'You said you had a ...'

But Collin didn't hear. His adrenalin was streaming. 'I loaded that confounded machine last night and I'm buggered if I'm doing it again tonight!'

I didn't like the way Meg was holding a saucer of their new dinner set.

*

But don't let me put you off. Marriage is interesting. No matter how well you think you know somebody ...

It started with tomato sauce. I could've sworn I had a spare bottle somewhere. It's worth stockpiling. The kids eat it with everything – sausages, eggs, cornflakes. They suffer withdrawal symptoms if I forget to buy it.

I flung open the cupboard most likely to contain a precious bottle. A large, well-filled, brown paper bag occupied most of the shelf and blocked my vision.

One thing I learnt early in life as a wife and mother is never look for more trouble than you've already got. The mysterious bag had nothing to do with me.

I poked around the side of it. No sauce bottles. I opened the next cupboard. It too was stuffed with a large brown bag. So was the next. The pot cupboard spewed lids and sieves over the floor when I opened it. Sure enough, tucked behind the frying pan, a large paper bag.

Perhaps this is it, I thought. At last. A well-earned rest in a mental home. I could see it already – 'Doctor, I can't go on! My cupboards are stuffed with paper bags!'

He would nod kindly, snap a hospital bracelet round my wrist and shepherd me to one of those liberal places where they let you do pottery.

I decided to avoid confrontation with the bags. We had dinner from the freezer that night.

'Where's the tomato sauce?' our older son asked.

'There isn't any.'

'Jeremy's mother gives him tomato sauce every night.'

The thought of Jeremy's mother grinning smugly in the post office queue roused strange emotions in me. Jeremy's mother and her perfect babies that never dribble. Her immaculate clothes that never get stained. Her endless tomato sauce supplies. No one would dare stuff her cupboards with – 'Who put all those bags in my cupboards?' I snapped.

My husband looked enigmatic. 'I did,' he said at last.

'What's in them?'

'Lemonade.'

The kids cheered.

'What do we want two hundred bottles of lemonade for?' I asked.

He shrugged. 'We've got years of birthday parties coming up.'

Perhaps he was the one who needed a holiday. Baked beans, as insurance against World War Three, could have been forgivable.

But lemonade?

'It's a competition,' he explained. 'I'm guaranteed to win. All I have to do is collect a label from each bottle to make up a code.' He produced a wad of cardboard labels from his pocket and began shuffling them the way Maverick used to on TV. 'When I get two more number 10s I'll win a watch. Or if I get five more number 7s I'll get a clothes dryer. Or three 12s for a calculator.'

'Isn't that sort of thing supposed to be for kids?' I asked.

'That's another reason I'm going to win. I've just been scrapping with a twelve-year-old down at the supermarket. I'm bigger than they are.'

It began to make sense.

I soon learnt lemonade was a versatile cooking ingredient. Lemonade soup, lemonade au gratin, lemonade cake. When friends came for dinner we'd ask 'Red or white?' If they wanted red, a little food colouring did the trick.

Time passed, but we were no nearer to becoming proud owners of a calculator, watch or clothes dryer. The labels, which my husband had pinned on the kitchen wall, curled at the corners and turned yellow with age.

'They must hold some of the key labels back,' he said grimly. 'I'll see if the supermarket's had a new load delivered. Maybe they've released the prize-winning combinations this week.'

Even the kids lost their taste for lemonade. They started begging for milk. I felt a shudder down my spine every time I saw a plump paper bag in the back of the car.

After a few weeks, the lemonade stream became a trickle. I didn't have the heart to remove the ancient labels from the kitchen wall. Sometimes I caught him gazing at them as if they were a lost love.

Then the other day I was looking for a particular bottle of fruit. I tried a cupboard. A chunky cardboard carton stared back at me. I opened the fridge. It was stacked with cardboard cartons.

'What's going on?' I asked.

'Beer,' he said.

'What?'

'If you collect enough bottle tops they make up a code, you see. And you win a car. Want a beer?'

WHAT TO DO WHILE THE LIGHT OF YOUR LIFE TURNS ON AT THE OFFICE

Life out here in the burbs is far from dull. If you're thinking the light goes out of our lives the minute our husbands head off for the city in the morning, I've got news for you.

There are heaps of things to fill in the day. Like wondering how many hours it'll be before he comes home again. You tend his house and babies with loving care.

Getting on for 6 p.m. you wrap yourself in a caftan and Dior. You put a romantic record on the stereo. It's crooning Jack Jones reminding you that just because you have a ring on your finger you needn't try any more.

You listen for the instantly recognisable drone of your family car.

Instead, all you can hear is Jack Jones warning that wives should always be lovers too. Run to his arms the moment he comes home to you.

In case you're not feeling a teensy insecure already, Jack drones on about the girls at the office who are so much prettier and more obliging than you are.

Just when you're about to tear Jack Jones off the turntable and hurl him at the Indian bedspread posing as a wall hanging, you hear your man's footsteps, the click of the door handle. The music reaches a crescendo – 'Time to Get Ready for Love' …

'Darling, you're home!'

'Who's been sick on the carpet?' he says. 'I can smell it.'

After a while, the routine gets a little unrewarding. You forget the caftan and Dior. Jack Jones makes way for Helen Reddy. I am woman. Hear me roar.

There's no point in trying to compete with the girls at the office anyway. They're in another world. Yours is peopled with characters you meet nowhere else. You'd better enjoy them. They're all you've got.

*

I saw him at the tip the other day. He was perched on a bulldozer. He wrestled angrily with the controls and jerked the thing into action.

Unaware of the seagulls whirling above his head, all he could see were mountains of rubbish. He was still scowling at the world.

The first time we met I was verging on tears. I had dropped the car keys down a drain. God knows how it happened. I was lifting the baby into the car one minute, then there was a jangle and an ominous splash. That was it.

I peered into the drain. Muddy black water glistened. It had engulfed the keys. A car without keys is a useless monument to technology. You can't do a thing. I was stranded.

I prised an amiable-looking taxi driver out of his cab. He stared down the hole and looked sympathetic.

Then he opened the boot of his taxi. It was filled with what at any other time would be useless junk. He made a primitive fishing rod with an unlikely collection of wires and pipes, stirred the mud like one of Macbeth's witches and dragged out a few strands of slime.

'I'm not getting anywhere,' he sighed. 'You'd better ring the council.'

I was shaking with panic when I rang from the garage across the road. I waited for what seemed hours. Then he came. He sprang out of the council van. A ball of bad temper. He was short and round under his grubby overalls. A haze of red hair hung over his face like a thunder cloud. He glowered at me, slammed the door and marched round to the back of the van.

'Sorry to drag you out like this,' I spluttered.

'Hmmph!' was all he said.

He drew out a long implement from the back of his van. It was like a spade with jaws. He inspected the drain with professional eyes. 'You haven't been stirring this, have you?'

'No.' My face was red with guilt. Technically it wasn't me who'd stirred it. The taxi driver would've described it more as fishing, anyway.

'If people go round stirring drains when they've dropped things down it makes my job twice as difficult.' He scooped up muddy water and inspected each foul load. 'You've got no idea what people drop down drains,' he snorted. 'Stupid idiots.'

I tried to mollify him. Men always like women to ask them questions. 'What sort of things?'

'Keys, mostly. Jewellery. It's women who do it. One woman dropped a string of pearls.'

He seemed to be getting near the bottom. With every scoop he released a deluge of stinking mud onto the curb. In it swam swarms of ice-cream sticks, plastic wrappers, soft-drink cans, cigarette packets and shreds of soggy paper.

But no keys. My optimism began to wane.

'Did you get the pearls back?' I asked, wanting reassurance more than an answer.

'Yep. All but two.'

It was a long job. His bad temper was not improving. Neither was the smell.

'Could swear this drain's been stirred,' he growled suspiciously.

At last a metallic sound.

A set of wet, rusty keys collapsed on the pavement like shipwrecked sailors on a beach.

He had to know the truth. I drew a deep breath.

'They're not mine.'

'What?!'

'I'm sorry. Somebody else must've dropped these. Mine are still in there. I'm sure.'

In truth, I wasn't so confident. His face contorted with fury. I thought he might hit me.

Time dragged on. He heaved a resentful sigh with every new load of filth. I felt wretched for destroying his sense of wellbeing. My presence irritated him profoundly.

To fill in time, I wandered over to the shopping centre. I tried to think of something that might make him stop hating me.

A bottle of aftershave winked at me from the pharmacy window. He'd need it after this day's work.

At last, the drain surrendered its treasure. My knight in overalls didn't seem any happier. I would have thrown grateful arms round him if he hadn't smelt so bad.

I handed him the flowery chemist's parcel. It looked silly and irrelevant. He eyed it as if it might be a parcel bomb. Then he grunted, thrust it in his pocket and stalked back to the van.

No doubt he was off to sort out some other idiot's crisis.

*

She was one of those women who make you think everything on the planet is alive and well. Not dressed too smartly, but neat and demure. A scarf latched round her neck. A hint of fading lipstick.

Her eyes were bright and humane. It was easy to envisage the hundreds of knitting patterns and *Woman's Weeklies* she must have pored over in her lifetime.

This was someone I understood immediately. I respected her devotion to her ideal of womanhood. She paid the price with little complaint, churning out cakes for school fairs, and roast dinners by the score. We were going to get on well.

We sorted through men's half-price T-shirts in a city department store. There was a pleasant hum of activity in the background. We were enjoying a temporary camaraderie.

'My son is really an XXL but if they are raglan sleeves he may be able to get away with a medium size,' she said.

I nudged a medium size in her direction.

'You can't really tell what sort of sleeves they are till you get them out of the packet,' she said.

The packet seemed impossible to open without causing permanent damage. We looked vaguely for a shop assistant. She continued her comfortable patter. 'Isn't it terrible these days? Nobody to serve you. No wonder they lose so much stock. Nobody cares any more.'

I nodded, and tore the bag open for her. I held the shirt up against myself to give her an idea of size.

'Oh, they're not raglan sleeves,' she said, disappointed. 'The last time I got him set-in sleeves like that they burst open. You see he uses them for pyjama tops. I make the trousers and he wears T-shirts for tops.'

I imagined her fifteen-stone progeny thrashing around in his T-shirt on a hot summer night. The seams strained dangerously. Any minute now and oops! Another half-price T-shirt down the drain.

'Why don't you get one for yourself?' she said. 'It's all the same these days.'

I looked in the mirror at the garment hanging limply against me.

It seemed intimidated by my womanly chest. 'It could be very useful,' she urged.

A thoughtful silence. Her eyes brightened and sparkled. 'Why don't you pinch it, dear?' she said.

'What?' I was convinced my hearing was on the blink.

'Go on,' she said, narrowing her eyes. 'Pinch it. Nobody's looking.'

Before I could say anything, she shrank behind a pillar, as if to say she wasn't going to look either.

I felt silly standing alone with the sad little garment I'd been instructed to steal. I peered around the pillar to see if she was still there. She was discreetly engaged behind the underwear stand.

I felt a surge of adrenalin. What if I followed her instructions and galloped outside clasping the thing to my bosom? They'd be bound to catch me. I'd feel such a fool.

'Could you please tell the court why you stole this T-shirt?'

'A nice conventional woman told me to.'

They'd think I was hallucinating.

I remembered the last time I'd yielded to that sort of temptation; I stole an eraser from Woolworths at the age of eight. I was so torn up with guilt that when I got home I ate the thing. Strangely, I gave up shoplifting and eating erasers on the same day.

I began to wonder if the woman was a figment of my imagination. I prised a shop assistant out of a dark corner and bulldozed him into selling me the thing.

'How much is it?' he sighed.

I looked for her as I went out the door. I felt I'd let her down somehow. She was nowhere around. Maybe she had to get home early to put the vegetables on for tea.

*

Salesmen. It's not very original to say they're a breed of their own. But it's accurate.

There's nothing like airing the family's continental quilts on a fine day, I mused as I dropped the bedclothes over the verandah rail to let them bask in a stream of sunlight.

I cast a proprietorial eye over the geraniums my husband had planted in the window box outside the dining room. They too seemed to be making the most of the watery sunshine.

After long periods of wetness, sunny days always brought out the wasps.

And door-to-door salesmen.

'Hello. I'd like to demonstrate this window brush,' a voice said.

I looked for the source. It seemed to be a hedge. Then a little man in a glossy blue suit appeared from behind the hedge.

'Where's your highest window?'

He clasped an extremely long stick. A mass of blue bristles

gleamed at the end of the stick, about a metre above his head. There was a coil of blue hose in his other hand.

'We haven't got any high windows.'

'Oh well. That doesn't matter. I'll demonstrate this wonderful cleaner on low windows.'

I knew I should be wary. 'How much is it?'

This proved to be completely the wrong time to ask a question like that. He seemed put out.

'Where's a tap I can plug this hose into?' he asked. He caught sight of our garden hose twisting over the patio and followed it into the depths of a flax bush.

'Other way,' I called.

I really should've been telling him to go the *other* other way. Out the gate and back to his van.

But then another man arrived. His brown suit was wrinkled like a paper bag. Both he and the suit had seen better times. He carried a substantial cardboard box.

'I've come to show you the carpet shampooer.' He beamed uneven yellow teeth at me.

'Carpet shampoo?' I said. 'I thought this was about windows.'

His mate was already halfway down the front lawn, clutching his cleaner.

'Turn on the tap, Fred!'

'Okay, Mike.'

Fred placed his carton on the driveway and disappeared with the line of blue hose into the flax bush.

Mike pointed the long, weapon-like implement at our dining-room window.

I dashed inside to shut it before the deluge.

'Watch out for my quilts!' I called, as if I was in charge of the situation.

He sprayed undramatic jets over the window. They dribbled down the glass into the flower box. Oh well. It was one way to water the geraniums.

'Now if I press this button you get detergent as well ...'

Rainbow bubbles appeared on the glass and streamed into the flower box. My geraniums! Their fragile petals were about to be smothered in detergent.

'See what a good job it does?' Mike was confident. Even though he looked slightly foolish standing three metres away from the window he was cleaning.

Fred strode down the lawn to admire his mate's work.

'Great!' Fred took two steps back and impaled himself in a most sensitive area. The culprit was a bamboo stick my husband had put there to steady carnations against the northerly blast.

Fred tried to regain his debonair-salesman appearance and snatched the sprayer from his friend.

The battle of wills over who should hold the thing set it spraying wildly over the garden – and my quilts.

'Now look how shiny it is,' said Fred, who'd won the match. Mike trudged up the lawn to the carton. I continued to admire Fred's efforts.

'How much is it?'

Fred gave me another grin. At least I'd asked the question at the right time.

'Thirty-seven dollars fifty!'

I took his card and brochures. I imitated a technique a teacher friend uses. Said I'd let him know if my husband could tell which window they'd cleaned when he got home. It worked. Male supremacy is still the name of the game.

I had a strong suspicion Mike was sulking. I wondered whether Fred had been fair, snatching the cleaner off him like that. He stood by the carpet-shampooer box with a dispirited air.

'How much is it?' I asked, as a form of comfort.

He opened the box to reveal a scientific collection of bottles and brushes. 'Fifty-two dollars twenty,' he said meekly.

I said I didn't think the shampooer would fit on my vacuum cleaner. He assured me it would fit any vacuum cleaner.

When I produced my battered, antiquated machine he decided the shampooer would fit any vacuum cleaner except mine.

Fred couldn't stand it any more. He charged into the living room brandishing a weapon that looked like an overgrown toilet brush. It was on a two-metre pole.

'How often d'you brush your walls?' he chirped.

'Not often,' I lied.

I'd never heard of people brushing their walls.

Sure enough, clouds of dust billowed from the wallpaper onto our heads. I considered buying something less substantial, a toothbrush maybe, to get rid of them.

I feigned interest in the brochures. As if to imply it would take a fortnight's study to glean deeper meaning from them.

Mike and Fred were beginning to lose heart. They hadn't felt the same about me since they'd seen my ancient vacuum cleaner. I clearly didn't have my priorities straight.

Fred used his last-ditch resort. A tubercular cough.

'You don't sound very well,' I said.

He smiled bravely – the way terminal cases do. 'It's nothing, really. Just a touch of flu.'

'You poor thing!'

'It's the heat that gets me.' He shot a beady eye at the kitchen. 'We have to cover this whole area this morning.'

Frankly, I was tired. Besides, I had the quilts to dry and bubbles to flush out of the geraniums.

Mike and Fred and their wares struggled out the gate. I hoped they'd find a happier hunting ground, complete with cups of tea, somewhere else.

*

Almost every tradesman I know has a serious health problem. George the plumber is assailed by regular attacks of tonsillitis. Trev the electrician has an intestinal condition.

It's hard to imagine why men who are as delicate as *la dame aux camelias* choose careers involving physical labour. They used to irritate me with their complaints and excuses – that is, until I met the carpet man.

Our old house was practically an icebox. We decided part of the problem was lack of carpet in the hallway. I had chilblains from traipsing down the hall at night to the bathroom.

Out shopping one Saturday, we unearthed a length of stunning turquoise broadloom on sale. We took it home and looked up Carpet Layers in the local rag.

An efficient-sounding woman (Eric's wife, I guessed) answered the phone. She said Eric would be over tomorrow to give us a quote.

Just after 10 a.m. the next day, Eric arrived, panting slightly after climbing the 105 steps to our front door. A lean, tall man with a widow's peak and dark overalls, he smiled shyly through heavy rimmed glasses.

I watched him stride across our naked floorboards. It was, he said, a straightforward job. His quote was reasonable. I liked him. He even offered to provide the underlay and promised to bring it with him the following morning.

I stayed home next day to wait for Eric. An hour after he was due, the phone rang. It was Eric's wife. She said Eric couldn't do our job today. He had a sore back.

Understanding how someone who spent his days bent over floors could suffer from occasional back pain, I offered what I hoped seemed the appropriate amount of sympathy.

She rescheduled him to arrive at our place next Tuesday morning. My husband wasn't impressed, but I assured him if we'd survived this long without carpet in the hall we could last a few days more.

Late Tuesday morning, there was still no sign of Eric. His lack of reliability was starting to irritate me. I was about to head out when the phone rang. It was Eric's wife saying his back was still bad.

I bit my lip and said, 'Oh really?'

She said he'd be fine by Friday afternoon next week.

I stayed home Friday afternoon, but Eric didn't show up. There wasn't even an apologetic phone call. What made Eric think his time was more valuable than mine?

I rustled in my handbag and dug out his quote. Alongside his signature was a phone number printed in small black letters.

After several rings, the familiar female voice answered the phone. I asked if Eric had any plans to come back to our place and do the job.

No, she said. Eric had suffered a heart attack on Wednesday. He was dead.

HOW SOON CAN HE GO TO BOARDING SCHOOL?

I remember gazing fondly at my newborn baby's face and thinking: 'How soon can you go to boarding school?'

There are galaxies of space between birth and boarding school. It took a while for me to become accustomed to this brand new person's relentless company. During the next five years, he was going to need me more than anything else. In return, I needed to acquire a Zen master's ability to never need him back.

*

The queue for *Star Trek* was too long. Besides, if I had to be shut in a cinema on a brilliantly sunny afternoon I preferred a nostalgic glimpse at James Bond.

'I want to go to *Star Trek*. It's better.'

There's something special about going out with your kid. Just him and me. Especially when he's six and starting to be civilised. We beamed approvingly at each other as the bus glided past the *Star Trek* cinema. I hoped he didn't notice.

'What's *Moonraker* about?' I asked. Kids always know what movies are about before they've seen them.

'It's just a man who's got lots of fillings. He runs away from a space fort and shoots other people. They keep shooting each other in the back for fun.'

'Don't pick your nose.'

'It feels good. Didn't you do that when you were little?'

After stopping at the Nibble Nook to load up with popcorn and ice cream 'like all the other kids', we stumbled into the cinema. Momentarily blinded, I allowed my senses to adjust to that powdery disinfectant smell peculiar to theatres and taxis. Gloriously gaudy carpet dazzled our eyes.

The audience consisted of squirming kids clutching bags of sweets and chippies, chewing gum and peanuts.

A day at the beach would've been better.

We scrambled over small, writhing bodies to our seats. Faded advertisement slides flickered across the screen. Can't kids ever sit still?

The soundtrack was punctuated with the thud of seats, lolly paper crackles and high-pitched chatter.

At last, the main feature started. Nothing could be further from real life than James Bond with his harem of beautiful, obedient women wearing lipstick that never fades.

'This next bit is good,' a voice piped up behind us. 'Just watch. The dogs are going to eat her … see? And now …'

Just our luck to sit in front of a couple of professional summer-holiday movie-goers.

James Bond was thicker around the middle and thinner on top these days. It's amazing he survived the seventies. Where did he find all those unliberated women half his age? His condescending patter is enough to get his face pushed in at any supermarket. Let alone in the glamorous world of spies.

The pretty blonde shop assistant didn't give James a second glance. 'Can I interest you in anything?' she asked.

He sneered lecherously at her. 'I'm tempted to say yes, immediately. But I'll look around first.'

Why didn't she hit him? Or did she disappear out back to throw up?

A psychiatrist would have a field day with James. Latent homosexuality is the obvious diagnosis. Anyway, despite an apparent obsession with his watch, he found plenty of brainless chicks to collapse gratefully underneath him.

When he lunged passionately at bimbo number three's mouth, the prepubescent audience grew restless. They wanted the killing to start.

'She's eating him!' a kid gasped in horror.

'Last time I had a marshmallow was at camp,' my kid added thoughtfully.

I glanced down and noticed he'd devoured the entire tub of popcorn plus the ice cream.

Just as James was heading off to Rio, my kid found a half-eaten chocolate bar under his seat. I hissed at him not to eat it, but it disappeared.

'I feel sick,' he groaned.

'Look at the beautiful women.'

'I'm glad they're not my mum,' he said loud enough for half the cinema to hear. 'They're so smart, I'd be shy.'

A ghastly smell wafted round the hot, restless cinema. Other people's kids were revolting.

My son pulled my ear down to his mouth.

'I breathed through my bottom,' he whispered.

*

We were a family in crisis. An anxious group circled the invalid. 'Please tell us now,' my husband said. 'Is it serious?'

The expert continued his examination, avoiding our desperate stares.

'I'm afraid we'll have to take it away for a week or two,' he said.

We recoiled in shock. Two weeks seemed light years away. The expert and his assistant wrapped the television in quilted plastic and carried it out the door. We stood at the living-room window and watched them lift it into the van. The dog leapt on the sofa and emitted a whine. As each of us sank into a bubble of private grief I was reminded (quite inappropriately) of my grandmother's funeral. Admittedly, I was only six when she died and had no appreciation of the deeper significance of the event.

'It's a nice evening,' I said brightly. 'Let's go for a walk.'

'But it's *Mickey Mouse Club* time and we never go out then,' Six-year-old whined.

I marched them round the neighbourhood. Haunted echoes from other people's televisions wafted from houses. The kids looked at me reproachfully.

'We didn't have a television when I was your age,' I said. 'We had to make our own entertainment. Let's go home and have a singalong around the piano.'

They weren't interested. Kids these days don't have strong leg muscles. You don't use them to watch television. The walk didn't last long.

I switched the radio on. A dash of classical music would do them good. But their little faces were blank and joyless.

Then one of them lit up. 'I know that song!' he said.

'Really?' I was amazed his taste extended to Mozart.

'Yeah. That's the car advertisement on TV.'

By Day Two they were irritable and biting their nails. When I asked what they'd been doing with their friends at school they said nothing. They were social outcasts because they couldn't talk about last night's programs.

They even stopped asking for things. They'd forgotten the latest toy that children should be blackmailing their parents into buying.

Day Three and we were into books. Remember those things with covers and paper pages? I actually found a few stashed behind the rubber plant. We had a nostalgic time turning all those pages.

There were no moody arguments about which channel offered more suitable viewing for preschoolers. No frantic rushes from the kitchen to turn off some bloodcurdling scene – the worst of which they'd already witnessed.

They stopped waking in the night screaming Dr Who was coming to get them. After a few more days, we were beginning to survive without television. I started to see those ghastly 'actually we don't have television at our house' people in a new light. (Though the fact that they say that after I've spent a good five minutes describing an exciting development in some serial is still unforgivable.)

I decided that when the television returned we would enter a new phase of discipline and reason. We'd sort through the program schedule each week and make democratic decisions about what we would watch and what we would turn off.

At last, the day arrived. The white van stopped outside our gate and the men struggled into the house with the rehabilitated monster. We gave them a tumultuous welcome. They beamed back at us like Greek heroes as we thanked them with grateful, shining faces.

The set was returned to its throne. It stared at us blankly. One of the kids rushed feverishly to press the 'on' button.

'Wait a minute!' I called.

It was too late. They were already into *Tarzan* so deep it would have been more trouble than it was worth.

*

I want my kids to grow up honest, well-informed citizens. So I lie to them – for as long as I can get away with it.

'If the chicken we eat isn't the fluffy chicken animal that runs outside, what *is* the chicken we eat?' he asks.

If it wasn't seven in the morning and I'd had a better night's sleep my brain would be out of neutral.

'Oh, just stuff from a factory.'

'What sort of factory?'

'I don't know.' Which is dreadful coming from someone who insists on intellectual rigor in all aspects of life except maths, homework and cryptic crosswords. 'Want a pancake?'

'Well, what meat is *real* animal – pork, beef, lamb?'

'Would you like syrup or sugar on your pancake?'

I have every right to lie to them. As their mother, it's my job. If they're going to believe what I tell them about Father Christmas and the Easter bunny, a chicken meat factory is hardly a stretch. Though I have to admit things *did* get out of hand with the Tooth Fairy.

'I haven't heard from Rose for ages,' he sighed over his pancake.

Rose, his personal Tooth Fairy, should never have been allowed to happen. It started when he decided to write to the Tooth Fairy. It seemed a sweet, harmless thing to do. He left a note with a drawing on his bedside table, and naturally the Tooth Fairy replied. The handwriting was in whimsical loopy letters and rather attractive if I say so myself.

What I hadn't counted on was the flood of return correspondence from the child who wanted to know everything, including the Tooth Fairy's name. Once Rose had a name, she sprouted a personality. Rose lives in Fairyland, of course, which humans can only visit in their dreams. Her hobbies include pollen dancing with her best friend Jasmine, who's waiting in the wings to be Tooth Fairy to his younger brother when he starts losing his teeth.

'I left a letter by my bed three nights ago and she still hasn't answered.'

'Maybe a lot of children have lost teeth lately,' I said. 'Is it on blue paper?'

'Yes and I did a picture of a bear for her.'

Did he know? Was he testing me? Would he have a nervous breakdown when he discovered the truth about Rose? A wave of weariness washed over me. I wasn't sure how much longer I could keep this up. It's a wicked world out there, full of cruelty and fear. A child deserves a fantasy world to escape into. Maybe I'll summon up the nerve to tell him on his wedding day.

'She might write to you tonight. Are you ready for school? Did you brush your teeth?'

He nodded and smiled.

'No, you haven't! Those teeth are yellow. Don't you *ever* lie to me!'

IF THIS IS A BARGAIN,
I'D RATHER PAY FULL PRICE

Has anyone seen my fur coat?'

'It's Wednesday, Mum.'

'What's that got to do with it?'

'It's the day we take used clothing to school for Saturday's fair, remember? I don't want to take just any old junk.'

'What happened to that bottle of French wine I had in the fridge?'

'Yesterday we had to take something they could raffle.'

I wondered what had happened to our copy of *The Joy of Sex*. No doubt it'd disappeared on book day. I hoped he'd erased our name in the front and the underlined bits.

Our highly socialised rubber plant disappeared for plants and produce on Thursday. Nobody had spoken to a piece of vegetable as much as we had to it.

Friday, I caught him casting an appraising eye over the oven.

'We have to take a used toy today,' he explained.

'Your school is not having my stove,' I said. 'I'm having enough trouble saving to buy all our stuff back on Saturday.'

He scuttled out of the kitchen and yelled, 'The stove was too heavy anyway. This toaster fits in my school bag just fine.'

More begging letters arrived on pink newsprint. Any vegetables, heirlooms or white elephants?

The dog must've known what I was thinking. She shot behind the sofa, leaving a vapour trail of silver fur.

I polished the knife on my skirt and marched to the vegetable patch.

'Stop!' my husband screamed. 'I've nurtured those cabbages from infancy. You can't kill them now.'

'I had no idea they were purely ornamental.'

'Let me see them through to a comfortable middle age at least,' he sniffed as he led me to the garage. 'There are plenty of white elephants in here. Like this three-legged chair. Who'd want that?' He loaded it into the car.

'We can't offload that awful stained high chair! Or that broken pushchair! What'll happen if someone finds out that ghastly picture of Mount Egmont came from our house?'

He ignored my pleas and drove off with the lot.

Saturday. I huddled by the school gates until they opened at 10 a.m. I galloped to the used clothing stand and lunged at my fur coat.

'How much?' I snapped.

'Well, it's a bit tatty and out of date. Five dollars will do.'

'Five dollars!' My precious coat was going for five dollars?

'Well, four if you like.'

The rubber plant was screaming for help among some ferns. 'Hang on!' I called. 'I'll save you!' It cost a dollar.

I struggled towards the toaster on the white elephant stand. 'Sorry, we're so busy,' the lady said. 'There's just been this terrible fight over a beautiful picture of Mount Egmont.'

'The toaster!'

'What, this broken-down old thing? Terrible the junk people load on fairs, isn't it? You might as well take it, dear. It looks lethal to me.'

As I headed back towards the car I came across a gladiatorial battle over our three-legged chair.

'Eight dollars!' an old lady screeched.

'Ten!' bellowed a man.

I followed the high chair and pushchair out the gates.

'Great bargains, they were,' the woman smiled. 'Twenty dollars the lot.'

*

I'm not ashamed to say most of our furniture came out of the For Sale column. Old stuff has soul, and there's nearly always a story attached.

'Remember when you electrocuted yourself on that fourth-hand stereo?' I'll ask him.

'What about the garden tools you bought that turned out to belong to our next-door neighbour?'

I'd been after a desk for some time. They'd always been too expensive or snapped up before I got there. This one was advertised, along with a settee and a table with cabriole legs. The desk was thirty dollars and still on the market. My pulse raced.

'Hang on!' I shouted down the phone. 'I'll get there as quick as I can.'

I leapt in the car and hurtled towards the other side of town.

One red light, two close shaves with pedestrians and several frantic map consultations later, I was there.

My heart sank when I saw a house with a thousand steps. I could make out a small family group slogging valiantly up the hill.

A pain shot through my chest. Were they after the divan, the cabriole legs or could it be … my desk!

I estimated a straight line through the bush and charged up, determined to beat them. I battled the muddy slope. Halfway up I hit the path and collapsed on a step.

'Hello,' a friendly voice said. 'Nice day.'

They were already on the way down. The man balanced a table on his shoulders with cabriole legs protruding like a pair of ears.

I plodded the remaining path and assailed the front door with urgent knocking.

'Yes?' The house owner looked me up and down as if he'd had a visitation from the Planet of the Apes. I gaped at my reflection in his hall mirror and quickly tore blackberry fronds from my hair.

'The desk …' I panted.

He looked dubious about letting me in. I tried to seem indifferent. Eventually he led me to the desk room.

'How many owners?'

'Just me and a little old lady who wrote letters on Sundays.'

His phone was ringing plaintively. Other buyers were hot on my heels.

'I'll take it.'

Taking it didn't turn out to be that simple. We humoured a friend with a trailer and a car with a tow bar. He paled at the sight of the house perched on high.

It wasn't the hill that did it. The desk was determined to stay in its old home. It refused to fit through doors.

After what seemed hours of cursing and obscure mathematical calculations, the men found a solution.

'Don't be so disgruntled,' my husband said as he carried what was left of my desk down the hill. 'Some people would do anything to own a desk with no legs.'

*

Sometimes I regret not buying a brand new sewing machine with a fancy two-year warranty. But it's probably just as well.

My mother and Aunt Lila were expert sewers. Mum outfitted us all beautifully when we were growing up. One of my early memories is of her treadling away at the old Singer. It had a gentle, human rhythm, like a heartbeat, but Mum said it was too slow. After a while she upgraded to one that could be attached to the electricity grid. Whenever she pressed her thigh against a lever it emitted a terrifying roar. Mum tried to teach me, but I was too scared of the thing. Sewing machines have always hated me.

But with the mortgage to worry about and a body that never fits any particular size offered in clothing shops, I decided to try sewing again. I was determined to make something that people wouldn't smile wryly at and say, 'Made it yourself?'

I bought a pattern for what seemed the simplest outfit – brown trousers and a floral top.

The machine practically chuckled with delight as I lugged it out of a cupboard. 'What's for starters?' it seemed to hum. 'An inside-out seam? Or would you rather I connected a trouser leg to an armhole?'

My hands went clammy. I plugged it in and waited for the usual purple smoke, ominous electric smells, and blue sparks.

All those tortured sewing-machine years flooded back. I spent two years unpicking drunken seams and inadvertently destroying school sewing machines.

By the time the graduation fashion parade came around, I had produced nothing wearable. Not even an oven cloth. In desperation, the sewing teacher appointed me commentator. Compared to sewing, it was a breeze reading out names while girls pranced about in front of their adoring parents and boyfriends.

When we moved to Homespun Grove and I met the playgroup mums, I learnt women could be obsessed with sewing machines the way some men are with their cars. When I told them I was making what amounted to a pant suit, the sewing machine one-upmanship began.

'I threw out the automatic multistitch years ago,' Sue said. 'Got an electronic, computerised with a digital clock now.'

'Mine's made out of the same metal they used in Skylab,' Bev chimed in. 'It's guaranteed by three astronauts.'

Their faces swivelled in unison to me. 'What's yours like?'

'Ordinary.'

'You mean it only does ecclesiastical tapestry and minor brain surgery?'

'Well, it does sew backwards, sometimes.'

They wished me good luck with the pant suit. I hurried home to curse and sweat over the machine.

Several hours later, I mopped my brow, gathered up pieces that were meant to be part of the outfit but somehow never made it and tried the thing on.

'What do you think?' I asked, completing a fashion model twirl in front of the kids.

'Gee, Mum. Those are great pyjamas!'

*

My interest in bargains seldom pays off. If I buy a pair of half-price shoes, I invariably arrive home with a different size for each foot.

My disillusionment with mainstream hairdressers began about a year ago. It wasn't so much their prices or the helplessness I felt trapped in their chairs. (What do they *see* from up there? Creepy crawlies in my scalp?)

The turning point happened in our local salon when a sixteen-year-old trainee told me to go blonde. I've always had a problem with self-styled beauty experts. They have such authority in their voices I invariably let them do what they want.

As she mixed a pot of evil-smelling goo I wanted to yell 'Stop!' But it was too late. She began combing the muck through my hair.

'I won't leave it on too long,' she said nervously. 'Things can happen with this stuff.'

Gripping the armrests, I listened to the fizz of chemical reactions. My scalp was on fire. I tried to calm my nerves by sifting through the dog-eared magazine she'd handed me, but it was no use. After what seemed hours, she took me to the basin and doused my head with freezing water.

'Oh dear!' she said, rinsing the last suds down the drain.

'What?' I asked. 'Has my hair gone blue? Am I bald?'

'Nothing like that,' she said with a careless laugh. 'It looks like your hair's exactly the same colour it was before. I don't know, maybe it'll look different when it dries out ...'

I should have been assertive and refused to pay, but I was so relieved to look my dowdy old self, I was grateful to empty my purse and leave.

Soon after, I noticed a customer in the pharmacy with a hairstyle that gave the impression she'd been assaulted by a blunt lawnmower. The uneven fringe and spikes gave her a touch of punk. She was hunched over the counter begging the shop assistant for something to straighten it out or curl it up.

'I wouldn't change it,' I said. 'It's a great look.'

'It's the two-dollar haircut woman,' she said, turning to me, pink with exasperation. 'She'll do the whole family, including the dog, for next to nothing. But look at *this*!'

I assured the woman I liked her hairstyle and asked for the two-dollar haircut woman's number.

The following Saturday, a battered Volkswagen toiled up the hill and parked outside our place. A fierce-looking, grey-haired woman emerged from the car. She heaved a large black bag from the back seat, marched through our front gate and hammered on the door.

'I didn't know anyone lived up here,' she said, gazing through the mist to the gorse across the road. 'Bit of a recluse, are you?'

'Not by choice,' I said.

She narrowed her eyes and peered at me. It was hard to tell if she was examining my bone structure or searching for signs of instability. She asked what the smell was. I told her my husband was cooking lamb stew.

'Put the kettle on,' she said, taking a mirror from her bag and propping it on the kitchen table.

She accepted the mug of tea I brought her. She pointed at a kitchen chair. As I sat down, she produced a plastic tablecloth and pegged it around my neck.

'How do you like it?' she asked, running a red plastic comb through my hair.

Well, sort of shaped round here, not too short on the top and just a little …'

A pair of scissors flashed in the light. She was halfway through the haircut already. My husband appeared in the doorway and watched with amusement.

'Turn that down!' she yelled.

I jumped nervously from my seat.

'Sit still! I'm talking to *him*,' she said, turning to my husband. 'Young man, you've got that stew on too high. You're going to burn the bottom of your pot.'

There are several things in life which are certain.

One is, if my husband does any cooking, it's always with the elements turned on too high. Another is, if I try to tell him, he'll never listen.

'Really?' he replied meekly. 'Just a minute. You mean, down to a simmer, like this?'

I could hardly believe it.

She eventually gave up trying to even my fringe near the horizon of my forehead and scalp. I tried to imagine the hiccough in the middle was characterful. She sheared one child. The other refused to come out of his bedroom.

'It'll be you next time,' she threatened my husband as she went out the door. 'And remember what I said about that stew.'

'Yes, thanks. I will. I never realised I was doing it the wrong way.'

I didn't need another haircut for a while. When I did, it was almost impossible to get a booking. Word was out about the two-dollar haircut woman. The whole suburb was starting to look like David Bowie.

NOSTALGIA IS A SILVER BUTTON

Sometimes, the mist and redwood fences of Homespun Grove would get too much for me. I loved to escape with the kids and show them my real home – the place where I grew up.

It was good to see the old town again. The traffic lights seemed to take a breath before they changed colour. I could feel my nerves ping as they slowly unwound. Back in the hometown it was easier to sit still and harder to move.

Buildings from my childhood were still there, though smaller. Only the trees had stayed the same size. Some of the faces were the same, but older.

Our visit was steeped in nostalgia. I went to the movies and – joy of joys – somebody actually rolled jaffas down the aisle.

The whole town still turned out for Friday-night shopping. The night air was electric with schoolgirls dressed up to the nines, and boys in their beat-up cars dragging up and down what's left of the main street. Most of it's been turned into a mall.

My life had turned somersaults since I ran away so ungratefully from this town. If the open-faced optimist who left this place had morphed into an exhausted neurotic it was no one's fault but mine. I went to a shop I used to frequent twenty years earlier and found it comforting – the button stand was still exactly where it used to be.

Warming to nostalgia, I wondered if lime milkshakes in metal beakers still tasted the same. I hurried along to the milk bar only to find it'd been turned into an industrial-style hamburger place. They hadn't even heard of lime milkshakes. I settled for chocolate froth in a cardboard cup.

The beach was savagely beautiful and deserted as ever.

Wind belted up my nostrils and the sea glittered. I plucked a few plump mussels off some rocks to take home to Mum. No pollution here. Well, not much, apart from a wisp of brown foam on the sand.

Locals seemed to take their luscious parks and gardens for granted. The days were longer here, the air warmer, life easier.

Mum and Dad weren't getting any younger. I missed them living so far away, and the boys adored them. I'd leave Homespun Grove in a breath if I could.

Outside the post office, I bumped into a younger friend. I'd heard she'd been unemployed since leaving school three years ago. When I asked what she'd been up to she said nothing much.

'Still go to those Saturday night dances at the Trades Hall?' I asked.

'Nah, they've turned it into a nightclub. There's dancing in the pubs but I'm still underage. We go sometimes, but the cops boot us out.'

I tried to avoid the question but it slipped out during an awkward silence.

'Got a job yet?'

'Nope.'

'What do you think you'll do with yourself?'

'Dunno. There's nothing to do in this stupid town. I'll be heading to the big smoke soon.'

*

Whenever I visit my hometown, I always make a point of driving down the hill past the old house. It was the setting for an unusual upbringing. My parents hadn't planned to live in a two-storeyed wedding cake complete with gothic tower. They'd put in an offer on a perfectly sensibly stucco house when suddenly their lawyer jumped the queue and snared the stucco house for himself. He told them not to worry. There was a perfectly nice Italianate monster down in the gulley that used to belong to a couple of eccentric ladies.

With rolling lawns and infinite hiding places, it was the ideal spot for Mum and Dad to undertake their version of parenting – long periods of neglect disguised as freedom, interspersed with intense bouts of inspirational teachings of Dr Spock meets Rudolph Steiner genre.

'Don't neglect your talent,' Mum would say, drop dead gorgeous in her red lipstick through a shroud of cigarette smoke. 'It's the best story in the Bible, the man who threw away his talents and regretted it.'

While Mum hadn't exactly neglected her talents, she'd definitely compromised them for us, her demanding though not meaning to be, family. If it hadn't been for us, or the War, she'd have gone to England and become a famous contralto like Kathleen Ferrier – not sewing another outfit for the Standard Two fancy dress ball.

Mum was never happier than when starring in one of the Operatic Society productions. Her performance as Bloody Mary in *South Pacific* was legendary – though we'd have preferred her to be the sugary blonde who sang about washing that man out of her hair. As Mum stalked the stage in her blackened teeth shrieking 'You like, you buy!' a girl in front of us whispered, 'I'm glad she's not *my* mother!' My sister tried to hide under her seat.

Character parts were Mum's forte. She wasn't fully alive unless she was about to step on a stage somewhere. If there wasn't a decent role for a contralto that year, and no solo for her in Handel's *Messiah*, mists would gather around our gothic castle.

Dad was an unconventional choice of husband being thirteen years older than her and the town gas manager. 'How's the gas, Bill?' the farming cousins would ask. He had his way of dealing with the disdainful glint in their eyes. After they'd go back to herd their cows for the afternoon milk, he'd sit at the piano and pound out a Beethoven sonata, or head off in the car on his own for hours.

Dad had a reputation for being loony, but not bad enough for incarceration, because he thought coal gas was out of date. He was convinced the town should convert to natural gas from the offshore oil fields. Then he said maybe one day the whole country would run on natural gas. The Fuel of the Future, he called it. I felt deeply embarrassed and sorry for the guy.

If, on the other hand, he turned out not to be nuts, people wouldn't be able to gas themselves in the oven any more. Mum said it'd be a peaceful way to end it all, drifting to sleep with your head in the oven. Except, she said, you'd need a cushion because the bottom of the oven would be hard for your head to get comfortable on. Glancing around the living room, I wondered which cushion she had in mind. The crushed green velvet one with tassels or the linen one with Japanese birds on it.

She said gas ovens had been a logical choice for many glamorous and creative women thwarted by the demands of sewing fancy dress costumes. The ghost of the lovely poet Sylvia Plath hovered over Mum's shoulder nodding agreement. But Dad said they wouldn't be able to do it much longer. Natural gas didn't poison people like coal gas, he said. It's just explosive.

Life in the gothic castle seemed tenuous enough without things blowing up. During the night sometimes my upstairs bedroom rocked violently like a ship at sea. A giant's shadow would ripple across the wallpaper. Was it the dreaded Ning Nong who roared and chased me through my worst nightmares? The Ning Nong was a giant yellow robot with a terrifying resemblance to the grader that combed the gravel on our street every Tuesday. Its shadow grew larger and more scary – until it shrank to Dad's familiar shape.

'Don't be frightened,' he'd say. 'It's only an earthquake. The river dragon lashing his tail.'

Even the mountain that stood sentinel over my cousins' dairy farms wasn't everything it pretended to be. People said its near-perfect cone meant it was a volcano waiting to have a tantrum. One day we might wake up in its boiling vomit and I'd be turned to stone on the kapok mattress, just like one of the people in Mum's library book about Pompeii.

Once in a while, I'd risk bringing a friend home. A girl called Maureen looked like she'd stepped into a haunted castle. I wished we were just an ordinary family in a rectangular house with Venetian blinds and gladioli. We tiptoed past Mum in the kitchen rehearsing her role as Katisha in *The Mikado* – 'Alone and yet alive!' – upstairs past my sister's bedroom exuding strains of Engelbert Humperdinck, and my brother experimenting with his chemistry set on the upstairs verandah … then into his bedroom where we climbed the ladder to the tower … home to my white mice menagerie.

The little rodents stank horribly and wouldn't stop copulating. Looking back, I feel guilty about the terrible pong they inflicted on my brother in the bedroom below. In fact, I've no idea why my parents didn't ban them altogether. But the house already sheltered a range of wildlife, from bees in the attic to wild cats in the basement. Maybe they figured a few hundred white mice wouldn't make much difference.

After Maureen and I scribbled a giant picture of our favourite Beatles, John and Paul, in red biro on the tower's wallpaper, knowing we wouldn't get into trouble because my parents weren't like that, Maureen showed me how to kiss a boy, using a pillow for demonstration. It looked unrewarding, even with someone like John. As I lowered my lips onto the pillowcase, the tower shook with a tremendous bang.

'Help!' we heard Mum yell from the verandah below. 'Your brother's blown his eyebrows off!'

*

Dad often wore a black jacket with silver buttons. It used to hang on a hook behind the bedroom door or drape soullessly over a chair.

There were always pens and pencils in the breast pocket. Pastel-coloured bills lined the inside pockets. When I was little he'd let me draw on the back of them with one of his pencils.

I secretly preferred paper that didn't have writing and figures on one side. But the privilege of using something that was his was so great I never let on.

That jacket reeked of coal from the gasworks he disappeared to each day, and soap. The smell permeated the scraps of paper, too.

I was about four when I got lost in a queue at the cinema. Bawling, I at last found a black jacket with silver buttons. I dived at it and grabbed his hand.

There was unfamiliar tension in the hand. I looked up. The head in the sky above the jacket wasn't my father's. It was the first time I'd ever really wanted the earth to bulge up and swallow me.

Mum, my brother and I were extroverts, but Dad needed time alone. On vivid sunny days, he'd stride across the front lawn with his hedge clippers, whistling Mahler.

I've never known anyone else who whistled Mahler. The choice of an emotional composer suited my father. Sometimes he seemed remote, brooding for days over some unspeakable problem. Yet he was capable of great tenderness.

When I was sick home from school he'd drive back from work to visit me at lunchtime. There'd be a book of cardboard press-out dolls or a colouring-in book under his arm. His blue eyes shone and there'd be endless gentle chatter. He knew what it was to be eight and sick.

After that, I embarked on a stormy adolescence and no longer knew what to say to him. It had been so easy before.

Nowadays, Dad and I grab Christmas and hurried visits to each other's towns to try and express things that were never said.

The blue of his eyes has intensified with the years. Everyone thought he'd curl up and die when he retired but he managed to divert his passion to the garden – and a few carefully chosen friends.

'The thing about growing old,' he says, nursing in another row of lettuces, 'is not to romanticise the past.' The other challenge, he says, is to keep the horizon broad and not let your world shrink to petty obsessions.

An unlikely couple, we tour record shops. Punk rock throbs out at deafening decibels while we pick through Mozart and Beethoven in a remote corner of the store.

People stop us in the street and greet him as an old friend. After they've exchanged pleasantries and said goodbye, I ask who that was. He says he hasn't the faintest idea.

'Someone came up to me in the pub the other day and said, "I thought you were dead, Bill! Someone asked after you in the pub and I told him you were dead." What do you think of that?' We beam at each other over coffee in the Flamingo Milk Bar.

'Met an old school friend of yours the other day,' he says. 'Said he used to be scared of me because I used to wear a black jacket with silver buttons. Damned if I can remember the thing.'

*

Some memories make you pleased you don't have to go and relive certain things.

'Do you remember me?'

I lifted my eyes from the newspaper. The sight of her left me stunned, but I knew there was nothing to be scared of.

Do I remember you? Does anyone ever forget the face of a teacher who had what they call a profound effect? Everything about you is etched into my subconscious in the indelible colours of childhood.

Her prim face carried the weight of the years since I had last seen her. I could tell nothing drastic had happened during that time. The same old lines were engraved more heavily. As if experience had affirmed her original opinions.

Her eyes were still clean blue, the whites tinged with pink. Her hairstyle was the same too – though it was greyer now and perhaps not quite so manageable. There was no reason to be frightened. After all, I was a woman too, now. Not the nine-year-old she had taught all those years ago.

'Miss Saunders!' The newspaper collapsed in my lap. 'I often think of you.'

Do I ever, Miss Saunders. I remember how you made me go to school half an hour early twice a week. I'd sit at my graffiti-carved desk in a shaft of dusty sunlight to toil over the same blue-and-white gingham. I could never embroider my name in a straight, red line.

You stood over me in your grey pleated skirt while the embroidery cotton weaved its drunken path. 'For goodness sake, girl,' you'd clip. 'Order your thoughts. Unpick and start again.'

I never twigged about using the checks as a guide. It was unpick, unpick, until the white squares turned brown from sweat and the odd tear.

I loathed and feared you, Miss Saunders. But I admired you, and so wanted to please you. Your report cards were tough. I respected that. But every one of them ended with the comment 'Could do better'. I never met anyone who was so tidy about life. At the end of the year, you invited me to your house for biscuits. I felt like a confused, defeated wrestler who is asked to shake hands with his victor afterwards to prove there are no hard feelings.

Each biscuit was a perfect white circle with a square of chocolate placed exactly in the middle. I asked if they'd come from a factory. You smiled and said you'd made them. I could hardly believe it. I sucked one with humility and felt sick afterwards.

She switched on her ten-out-of-ten smile. 'I often think of you, too – whenever I have a problem child. Not that I mean it personally.'

Yes, I knew I was a problem, Miss Saunders. Honestly, I couldn't help it. I just couldn't fit into your mould.

You were Mother Duck, bustling with your flock of children. You were the centre of our solar system. I was the duckling who hung back in the distance, zigzagging after bright ripples on the surface. Likely, in your eyes, to be devoured by eels.

'I still remember how you jumped over the wooden horse in the gym,' I said. 'You flicked your feet up into the air and flew over without misplacing a single pleat in your skirt.'

She went momentarily pink with embarrassment – or could it have been pleasure? Then she suddenly became stern.

'You were a dreamer,' she said disapprovingly. 'I often wondered what happened to you. Do you have children?'

'No, I mean yes.' I could sense her irritation. ('Get your thoughts in order, girl!') Oh dear. I was just as bad as ever. 'Two, but they're not here at the moment.'

'What are they?'

I stared blankly at her. It was as if I'd shot back in time and she'd asked me eight times nine. I was sure she was tapping her foot.

'Boys?' she probed.

'Yes. Two boys.'

Something invisible hovered between us. I had the feeling she was disappointed. She had clearly expected more of me than child-bride motherhood. I tried to dredge the mature woman out of me.

'You're high up in a secondary school now, aren't you?'

'Well, deputy principal.' She lowered her eyes modestly.

Miss Saunders was tiny. I was mildly surprised she didn't wear the grey skirt any more. Or the sensible green suede shoes with tassels.

I asked if kids were any harder to teach these days. She said they weren't, but they were disillusioned. She put it down to the silicon chip and unemployment.

As we said goodbye beside the soldier lines of pot plants in her front porch, I could sense her disappointment.

Miss Saunders, I'll try and do better.

WELCOME TO MY NIGHTMARE

Tempted as I was to stay back in my hometown to raise the boys on Mum's cooking and milk from my cousins' farms, I couldn't see a future there. For all its drawbacks, at Homespun Grove I was technically an adult.

To prove it to myself I invited six people over for dinner – and regretted it immediately. It was a reckless move for someone who could hardly boil an egg.

Out in the kitchen, I was sweating over three different sauces, a casserole that was burning its bottom and a stack of dishes that had forgotten to wash themselves after breakfast.

Every now and then, I wiped my hands on my apron and pressed my ear against the wall to hear how our guests were getting on in the living room. Nobody had committed murder so far.

'Everything all right in there?' someone called cheerfully through the door.

'Yes!' I shouted, pummelling lumps out of the gravy.

The guest poked her head round the door.

'Slaving away?'

A scorched smell filled the air. The pot of white sauce swelled up and hissed over its rim onto the element.

As I snatched up the pot, a dollop of sauce rose into the air and spilt over my chest. I doubled up and cursed. The guest interpreted this as a signal to move closer.

'Are you sure you don't need help?' she asked, adjusting her silver shawl.

'No, no! It'll be ready soon.'

The white sauce looked like baby vomit cascading down my black dress. I dabbed it with a dishcloth, making it settle into a stain the shape of Australia. The guest watched owlishly as I opened the oven door and scooped the crust off the burnt casserole into another dish.

'New recipe?' she asked. It was impossible to tell if she was being ironic. 'There must be *some*thing I can do …'

I told her to set the table.

'Oh good! Where are the knives and forks?'

'Top left-hand drawer.'

I heaved the burnt casserole dish onto the pile of grubby breakfast plates, which sent an avalanche of crockery clattering to the floor.

'*Which* left hand?'

I had no idea what she was talking about.

'Do you mean the left hand if you're facing the laundry or the dining room?'

'Dining room,' I said, shovelling a broken bowl into the rubbish bin.

'Over here?' she asked, pointing a scarlet fingernail at the drawer I use for lunch wrap, rubber bands and toys from cereal packets.

'No, *there*!' I snapped, reaching for the cutlery drawer and yanking it into my thigh.

The word I'd been trying not to use in front of the boys exploded from my lips.

'You're lost when it's not your own kitchen, aren't you?' she beamed. 'Where did you get these darling pottery mugs – make them yourself?'

The clock was ticking. Our guests were probably starving.

'I'll do it,' I said grabbing a fistful of spoons.

'No, *please* let me!' she said, scooping them from my hand and gliding serenely into the dining room. I gathered up forks, knives, side plates, condiments and butter and staggered in behind her.

'Something's burning.' She sniffed thoughtfully.

'No, it's just taken a while for the casserole smell to get in here.'

'But this is a *different* sort of burnt smell,' she said, swooping back into the kitchen. 'Is that custard? Oh, look! It's got little black bits in it. You should always watch custard. Got a wooden spoon?'

I started mashing the potatoes while she stirred the custard with maternal concern. A titter of laughter wafted from the living room.

'I'll just see how they're getting on,' said a male voice, coming closer. He opened the door and stared vacantly at the bombsite that was my kitchen.

'How're we doing?'

'Fine, fine,' I said, pounding another potato to death.

'Shall we hang on to our glasses, or what?'

'Get the wine glasses down from the top cupboard.'

'The ones with stems or the chunky ones?'

'Let me do it,' I said, lunging at a stool and slipping on some sauce I'd forgotten to wipe up. As I landed on the floor in a position that would be the envy of any yogi, another head appeared round the side of the door. 'Want some help?' he asked.

*

Then there was the Brownie.

'Quick! Clean up the house. The Brownie's coming!'

The day hadn't started well. The dog was munching muesli on the back doorstep. I'd only just stopped myself putting dog sausage in the kids' cereal bowls.

'But she's coming to tidy the house, Mum.'

'She can't tidy the house when it's in a mess like this.'

In a moment of weakness I'd agreed to test the Brownie for her House-Orderly Badge. Perhaps it was the irony that had appealed:

the street's worst housekeeper assessing someone else's ability to be orderly.

It wouldn't have been so bad if I hadn't discovered my old school reports stuffed in the back of a cupboard the day before. The ink scratched by term-weary teachers had faded a little. The impact had not.

Mr Jackson's 'The hoped for improvement in spelling and French has not yet come' still cut through me like a knitting needle.

Miss Thomson could keep her 'very fair' for maths. She'd hardly been 'very fair' throwing chalk at girls and calling them sluts.

It would have been more honest for some teachers to have put 'Can't remember this one' instead of a non-committal 'good'. Good for what?

The phys-ed teacher who signed a mysterious 'BC' knew who I was – 'Works well when prepared to use effort required'.

BC probably knew most of my phys-ed energy went into working out shortcuts for cross-country runs. And how to spend longer in changing rooms than in the gym.

School reports are a cruel reminder to kids that they're a low form of life to be inspected dispassionately – like semen samples.

Hungry for adult approval, I'd hung on every word those teachers had scrawled late at night when they'd wished they were in bed.

That's why the Brownie was getting to me. I knew she'd be thinking about me too, worrying if I'd be bossy, fussy or patronising.

Of course I'd pass her. She'd have time enough to learn about failure. But then the pamphlet from the Brownies had said to make sure the girl felt as if she'd had a proper test.

The morning paper was soggy from overnight rain. I brought it inside and put it in the oven to dry out at a low temperature.

When the Brownie arrived, I tried to make her feel at home and set her to work on the dining room, the only tidy room in the house.

Her bright-eyed enthusiasm put a lump in my throat. 'You're doing a wonderful job,' I said, hoping it didn't sound condescending.

She polished the table, cleaned the windows and swept the floor with painstaking attention to detail. My fingers itched to sign the piece of paper saying she'd passed.

But she wasn't going to let me off that easily. She said she had to wash a pair of socks as well. All the dirty socks were squelching around in the washing machine. I found a clean pair for her to wash.

When she'd finished, I asked if I could sign, but she said she needed to clean our bathroom sink.

At last, I seized her form and wrote swirls of approval under the section marked 'Comments'. The poor child was probably looking up to me as a queen of domesticity. I asked if she had any questions.

'Yes, Mrs Brown,' she said politely. 'Why are you cooking a newspaper?'

*

Gilbert and I were students together. A pair of misfits, we were almost in love with each other, but I had my sailor boyfriend and Gilbert was having enough trouble getting himself dressed for class. After that, we lost touch. I went off and got married, and Gilbert – well at least one of us stayed true to himself.

The other day, I answered a knock at the door, and there he stood. With his long hair, bare feet and backpack, he hadn't changed a bit. I was so happy to see him I flung my arms around him – then remembered Gilbert never washed.

'Hey, man, can I crash at your pad?' he asked.

Flattered and delighted, I welcomed him into the living room.

'Not a bad set-up,' he said, peeling off his backpack and unravelling a sleeping bag on the couch. I rested a hand on his shoulder and guided him to the spare room at the end of the hall. He stood in the doorway and cast a judgemental eye over the neatly made beds.

'You have a *spare room*?!' he said, sneering at the home-made hessian curtains, the macrame wall hanging and the copy of Desiderata yellowing inside its frame.

When I explained it was mainly for my parents when they came to stay he shook his head and said, 'That's mighty bourgeois, man.'

Did anyone really say 'man' any more? I wasn't sure which of us was more out of touch.

Gilbert flung himself on the bed, offering a full view of his feet. The soles were blackened and cracked.

'Hey, man, how much rent do you pay?' he asked.

'Well, the mortgage is about …'

His mouth twisted with scorn.

'You *own* this place?'

He sat up and peeled his toenails while I explained how I didn't understand the maths properly, but the bank owned most of it.

'Next you'll be telling me you've got kids.'

He raised his head at the sound of approaching thunder from down the hall. A small blonde head appeared round the door.

'Hey, Mum! Andrew's been sick on the carpet!'

Gilbert and the child assessed each other.

'What's that smell?' the child asked.

Over the following days Gilbert spent a lot of time incarcerated in the guest room. He preferred not to join us for meals. Instead, he scoured the fridge for leftovers in the middle of the night. He appeared in the kitchen at lunchtime to help himself to coffee and cereal.

My husband asked what Gilbert did all day. I said he was writing a novel, though going by the aroma wafting under his door, he was just smoking weed. My husband wanted to know how long Gilbert was staying. I had no idea. Thinking it was time Gilbert pulled his weight, I asked if he wouldn't mind babysitting one night. He said that would be cool – not that he or the boys were ecstatic about the prospect.

The thrill of going out to a movie was tempered by anxiety about Gilbert's childcare skills. When we arrived home, we were relieved to find the house darkened and serene under the glow of a streetlight. We'd underestimated Gilbert's ability with kids.

I slid the key in the front door and crept quietly towards the kitchen for a last cup of tea before bed. As I tiptoed through the living room, I stumbled over a lump on the floor. A pair of eyes blinked up at me.

Standing up, I flicked the light switch. Gilbert and two scruffy individuals were draped over the furniture. A third, Martin, was prostrate on the floor. Surrounded by half-empty wine bottles, some of which I recognised from my husband's burgeoning 'cellar', he smiled benignly at us. As his guests struggled to their feet, Gilbert complimented us on our stash. He'd found the reds particularly enjoyable.

Next morning, Gilbert and I stood at the front gate. A gust of wind rippled his hair. Outside, he didn't smell so bad. Or maybe he'd taken advantage of our shower. In his second-hand military coat, he resembled a dishevelled Napoleon. I tightened the strap of his backpack and felt a surge of the old fondness. For a brief moment, we were students again. A spark flashed between us.

'You used to be so alive,' he said gently. 'What happened to you, man?'

I couldn't find words to answer.

MY DOG HAS WHEELS

Most people's dogs have paws. Ours has wheels. Given the choice, our Golden Retriever, Rata, would while away the rest of her life in the boot of our hatchback.

I can't remember when she wasn't an integral part of the car. Though we tried to discourage her, we've had to accept our dog's right to choose. The moment she escapes the house, she gallops straight to our parked car to sit behind the back wheels and whine longingly up at the hatch. Sometimes, if we're not going out I take pity on her and let her sit in the back with the hatch open. She'll stay there for hours, staring over the front seats through the front windscreen, no doubt fantasising she's on a road trip across the Sahara.

When she accompanies us on an *actual* car trip to the supermarket or playground, people have no qualms expressing their opinions – especially hearty, dog-loving types who assume we've trapped her in there.

'That poor dog! Why don't you let her out?'

The woman's two fox terriers yapped at my ankles while I wandered around to the back of the car, opened the hatch and urged Rata to leap to freedom. The animal stared sphinx-like into the middle distance and refused to budge.

If dogs resemble their owners, Rata and I are the perfect match. We both lumber about on over-large feet and have a tendency to emit gas at unpredictable times. She'll eat anything, including paper bags, but when she looks up at me through those molten eyes, I can't tell her off. Rata has looked after the boys since they were babies. Besides, she's not stupid. I'd much rather sit in the car than chase those yapping, hyperactive idiots across the park.

The dog lover glowered and harrumphed off to the playing field, fox terriers in her wake.

Rata's inactivity has led to one problem which, as far as dog owners go, is inexcusable. Obesity. Her weight problem does, however, give joy to one section of the community. On the rare occasions she agrees to get out of the car and go out for a waddle, we're invariably stopped by plump matrons.

'What a fat dog you've got!' they say. My tongue gets sore with biting.

*

There are times when I'd rather be left alone. This was one of them. It was cold and wet. I'd spent the day toasting my chilblains on the heater. But around three o'clock, a tiny nagging voice started up in my head.

'That poor kid, trudging up the hill in the cold,' it said. 'Look at yourself, lying around inside while he's getting wet through after a hard day at school.'

I pretended not to hear. He had a raincoat, hadn't he? But on my way to the kitchen for the third piece of toast, I cast a guilty glance out the window. The rain was coming down like nails. I heaved the preschooler into the car. The dog invited herself on the journey as usual.

We pulled up outside the school gate to join the neurotic parents' brigade. There we all were, clustered in our cars, scared our kids might dissolve in the rain. Still, they arrive on earth in a strange enough fashion. It wouldn't be all that surprising if they disappeared in an equally freaky way.

I remembered all the occasions I'd walked home in the rain when I went to primary school. Thousands of times. In fact, it rained every day, if I remembered rightly. I never expected anyone to drive *me* home.

Still, there's something reassuring about being encased in a car in the rain. You're safe from interruptions because nobody would bother …

'Excuse me.'

The world's worst conversations start with those words. I hate them. They were coming from outside my window. I wound the knob and found a face in a rain-hood. Perhaps it was her beaky features or her sharp, go-getter eyes. Or maybe it was the deluge of rain that hit me when I opened the window. I didn't like her.

'Do you live in Homespun Grove?' Her voice was unpleasant. It had tension about it – like the wail of an air raid siren.

'Yes.'

She peered over the back seat. 'Is that your dog?'

Would we put up with the smell if it wasn't?

At this point, her rain-hood seemed to inflate slightly and the whites of her eyes went pink.

'I'm sick and fed up with that dog of yours fouling our front lawn.'

'Yes, but …'

'If it happens one more time, I'll phone the dog catcher.'

She was flushed with triumph. I was silent. I can never summon up a flow of words when I need them. If I'd had three brandies, I'd have come up with three perfectly stunning phrases. But then I would have fallen asleep. I tried to pull myself together. If I couldn't be articulate I could at least give a semblance of dignity.

'What number Homespun Grove are you?' I asked.

'Number twelve.'

'Then it can't be our dog. We live way up the top and she never takes any exercise past the front gate.'

She gave the animal another steely look. 'Likes children, does it?'

Trick question. 'Yes.'

'That's her then.' She stuck her jaw out. 'The dog that messes our lawn likes children.'

Women fight tough. I wished she'd go away. Why couldn't she build a fence around her precious grass? But I was too annoyed to string a sentence together.

'I won't put up with it any longer,' she sniffed. 'You'd better do something about it.'

She spun on her heel and flung another few gallons of rain in my face. The dog looked mournfully innocent in the back seat. I felt like moving into number fourteen and feeding the animal nothing but licorice for a fortnight. Frustrated, I went to a friend's house to lick my wounds.

'But it's horrible having a dog mess up your lawn,' she said earnestly.

I'd been hoping for sympathy.

'But it's not our dog.'

'We used to have that problem here. It was revolting. We even put up an electric fence to keep the dogs out. It didn't work. They seemed attracted to it more than anything else.'

I looked through her net curtains to a perfectly smooth green lawn.

'How did you solve it?'

'Well, you've heard the one about posting the offending material back to the dog's owner?'

'Yes.' I hadn't, but didn't want to interrupt her flow.

'I took things a step further. I scraped it into a paper bag and put it on their doorstep.'

I couldn't believe this was the normal, sane woman I knew. Her breathing had become fast and shallow.

'Then I set fire to the paper bag.'

'What happened next?'

'I rang the doorbell and ran away. A man opened the door and saw the little fire on his step.'

'Then what?'

Her eyes glittered with delight.

*

A strange thing happened in the supermarket car park one day.

I heaved two grocery bags next to Rata in the back hatch. She gave them an interested sniff as I walked around to the driver's seat and slammed the door.

As I was about to turn the key in the ignition, an earnest male face pressed against the window. He was pale and panting.

I spun the window down. His hot breath hit my face in waves. 'Are you interested in mating?'

'What?' I tried to repress a blush. This certainly was an unusual approach.

'She's not a bad bitch.'

'Who?' I glanced anxiously over my shoulder to see which world-worn housewife he was talking about.

'Your dog, of course.'

The dog. Such a permanent fixture in our car I'd forgotten she was there.

'Oh. She's been spayed,' I said.

'I can't understand why people get good dogs and have them sterilised,' he said, his face twisted with disappointment. 'Your dog's coat and my dog's head would've made a beautiful combination.'

I tried to explain our situation. We'd had a baby, then a dog to keep the baby company – instead of another baby. Then, owing to a faulty batch at some pill factory in Surrey, another baby arrived. A baby, a toddler and a dog were already beyond my capabilities.

'We tried to stick it out for a while,' I told him. 'Reminded ourselves how educational it'd be for the kids to have puppies.'

That was before she went on heat.

Demented suitors of all breeds and sizes appeared outside our place day and night. The fence kept most of them at bay. Only very small ones could squeeze under. They didn't worry me at first. What could they do to our lumbering golden retriever?

I soon realised what they lacked in size, they replaced with speed and cunning (rather like the short men I'd encountered in younger years). They lurked behind bushes and spent long hours ornamenting the garden.

Doberman and Alsatian types soared over the fence like impassioned pole-vaulters. Their egos were easily punctured. A stick and a curse would get rid of them, but only for a while.

The kids revelled in this home circus.

'Come and watch Mum fight the dogs,' they'd say to their friends.

In a reflective moment our older son asked why I was so cruel to Rata's friends. They only want to play trains.

My parking-lot companion nodded sympathetically as I finished the story.

'These days she thinks she's human,' I added. 'Refuses to go for walks. Just sits in the car all day or lies on the sofa watching soap operas.'

'It's the breed,' he said. 'They can be lazy, especially if they're overweight.'

'When we got her I didn't realise we'd be spending the rest of her life eating dog hair soup …' I said, ignoring his not-so-subtle criticism.

'Ah yes,' he said with a smile. 'I tell dinner guests it's a South American herb I sprinkle on everything.'

'Then there are vet bills, kennel fees, food bills, licence fees, worm tablets, shampoo … and I hate feeling unacceptable on beaches …'

The man kicked the concrete and said I'd put him off mating altogether. He sighed, stuffed his hands in his bush jacket, and disappeared into the shopping complex.

CHEWING IT OVER

It was one of those days. I climbed out of bed and sprayed oven cleaner under my arms. (What oven cleaner was doing in the bedroom was anyone's guess.)

I prepared a nourishing delicacy for the kids' breakfast. Baked bombe muesli served with 100 per cent pure orange juice ('Guaranteed genuine'). When I placed the masterpiece in front of them they screwed their faces up and said 'YUCK!' in unison.

Resisting the urge to throw the milk jug through the window, I asked what they felt like having for breakfast. The older one said hamburger and chips. His younger brother said lollies.

Later that morning, polishing the furniture with fly spray (the cans were the same colour) I wondered which would be more pleasant – death by sherry excess or valium overdose? A voice inside my head pushed the thoughts aside, warning I was turning into my own mother.

Later that night, they decided to cheer me up by taking me to a hamburger restaurant. I pondered their motives, but decided anything would be better than slaving over another meal only the dog would appreciate.

As we burst through the restaurant doors, the staff cowered behind the counter. Call yourselves a family restaurant? Well, here we are! A four-headed, eight-legged monster. The waitress found what she probably imagined was a discreet corner. She stood over us and fiddled with her hair while we studied the menu. Hamburgers and fries. Fish and fries. Fries and fries.

'I wanna milkshake!' the six-year-old yelled.

My eyes darted across to the other tables. Several customers, I could tell, thought he should have something else.

'You don't have to shout!' I said, trying to keep the tone even.

'Chocolate, vanilla or strawberry?' the waitress asked.

'Yeah,' the child replied.

'Which one?' she asked, shifting the weight on her feet.

'Chocolatevanillastrawberry.'

Fast food always seems to take so long. We waited. Three-year-old wandered off to collect cutlery from empty tables and stuffed it in his pockets.

'Come here!' I hissed, grabbing his hand. 'Don't do that!'

His scream left the whole restaurant in no doubt I was a child beater.

Six-year-old wanted to go to the toilet. Entering into the spirit, his younger brother downed his pants in an effort to save time and trailed after him towards the bathroom door.

The way I saw it, I had three options. A) scramble around tables and chairs after them in an attempt to preserve decencies. B) act as if they're not my kids. C) Pretend they were out of my sight line.

I opted for C. The meal, when it arrived, was barely digestible. The kids loved it. Three-year-old poured salt on his milkshake, sugar on his chips and devoured the lot. Six-year-old was so focused on his pile of chips, he nudged his milkshake with his elbow.

'Careful, you'll spill your drink!'

He ignored me and shovelled another pile of chips in his mouth. 'Watch out, you'll ...'

The glass scuttled across the table. A long finger of milkshake dripped onto the floor. I soaked up what I could with paper serviettes.

Heaving a sigh, the waitress produced a large bucket, mop and container of detergent. My apologies were accepted with a weak smile.

I frisked Three-year-old for remaining cutlery and we headed for the cashier. The meal was expensive enough not to make me *too* guilty about wrecking the joint. Still, I kept my head down to avoid accusing stares from customers and staff.

Young families and restaurants don't really equate. Our eight-legged monster creates less mayhem at home.

With time, someone will perfect the family restaurant. lt'll probably look like one of my cousin's milking sheds with a concrete floor for convenient hose-outs.

They might even offer a bring-your-own-straitjacket service – for parents only, of course.

*

Food is fascinating to the housebound woman. Lonely hours can be filled wondering if you're eating too much or not enough.

I'd been looking forward to the lunch for ages. The generously shaped hostess assured me we were in for a feast. I was reassured to see the other guests looked as if they too enjoyed their food.

We hefty women have a bond. Some of us try to fulfil the cliché of being jolly, but we're often sensitive and insecure.

Many of us admit we eat when we're lonely, worried, depressed or bored. It's not difficult to feel like that when most dress shops stock sizes only a tapeworm could wear. Glamorous outfits hang on pegs for the elusive skinny lizzie while the streets are full of curvaceous women like us.

Fashion tells us being skinny is the only way to be attractive and happy. Doctors harp on about heart attacks and obesity-related illness.

Meanwhile, fat people try to untwist a ball of emotions and habits in the hope food will stop being the primary method of filling the emptiness inside.

Sure enough, conversation at the gathering revolved around food. But it wasn't what I'd expected. They weren't exchanging recipes for rich sauces and puddings.

'Have you tried the Israeli diet yet?' the hostess asked. 'Nothing but apples for two days, then cheese the next two. That's followed by two days of salad and two days of chicken. Works wonders. Of course, you're only supposed to drink water but I cheated and had black coffee instead.'

I took a slip of paper from my handbag and pretended to take notes.

'I'm into Weight Watchers,' another Junoesque woman said. 'I'm going for one of those brooches with a diamond for each stone you lose. I've only lost a few pounds so far, but watch this space.'

We watched enviously while she tugged the elastic waistband of her trousers and flaunted a gap of at least half an inch.

'It's been months since I tasted a potato,' her friend sighed.

I was disconcerted to see the hostess nodding in fierce agreement as she disappeared into the kitchen. My heart sank when she returned with a tray of miniscule salad bowls and tuna.

'Oh, that's really too much for me,' the Israeli diet said, inspecting her salad. 'Just one piece of lettuce will do. You see, I'm on day five.'

'I shouldn't, but I will,' the Weight Watcher said. 'I'll go without dinner tonight.'

Spectres of glamorous, slim women hung over us as we nibbled silently, savouring each chomp of lettuce.

'Do you remember Elsie Townsend who used to work in the cake shop?' the hostess said. 'Well she lost five stone and went quite peculiar. She ran away with an Italian. Her husband and kids are devastated.'

The group murmured disapproval.

There was no evidence of a second course. The women emitted sighs of contentment. Still hungry, I thought maybe I'd have to stop at the petrol station for a chocolate bar on the way home. We sipped black tea thoughtfully. I couldn't believe we could eat so little and remain so large.

'They say Maria Callas never sang the same after she lost all that flab,' the Weight Watcher said sadly.

'Some people look better with a few extra pounds on them,' the Israeli diet added. 'My husband always likes his women chubby. He says they're more sensuous.'

The hostess quickly picked up the gist of the chatter and disappeared. When she returned with an enormous cheesecake, the relief in the room was palpable.

The cake was gone in no time.

*

Have you ever tried to chew a piece of food fifty times?

It's the sort of nonsense people told me to do when I was growing up. It wasn't till Professor Chee Soo brought the subject up in his book *The Tao of Long Life* that I thought about it again. After all, who doesn't want to live to be 150 or 200?

I sank my teeth into a piece of wholemeal bread, assuming it would be a suitable texture to sustain fifty chews. The first ten chomps were okay. By twenty the bread was decidedly watery and tasteless. At thirty I could stand it no longer and swallowed.

That evening I couldn't keep pace with the family meal. I was up to chew twenty-three of my first fork-load of bolognaise and their plates were nearly clean.

'Mum, where did I leave my socks yesterday?' (They think my life revolves around their socks.)

'Fifteen, sixteen, seventeen, eighteen …'

'What's the matter with her this time?' the kid asked my husband.

I'd become a devotee of the professor ever since he put me right about my thighs. You see it's been a lifetime ambition of mine to have a gap between my upper thighs when I stand with my feet together.

Though I'd come to accept that was never likely to happen, short of terminal illness or global famine, I occasionally felt a tinge of sadness about it.

The professor doesn't approve of those gaps at all. He says they're

Yin and a sign that the owner of the gap is over-emotional. In fact, he says many characteristics we in the West regard as beautiful are signs of bad health. That's why I'm so glad I haven't got a tall thin body, fat lips and eyelashes like shop window awnings.

I'm much healthier in my more Yang condition. Short and stocky with long thin eyes and a short, turned-up nose. Well, maybe I'm not as Yang as all that.

According to the professor, if you want to diagnose someone's health problems, all you have to do is study their face. I noticed the owner of our local dairy had a horizontal line between his upper lip and nose. His hair was frizzy – and split ends! That, combined with his dark lips, left no doubt. The poor man was stricken with unhealthy reproductive organs.

But I'd just discovered that very morning I had schizophrenia. Bizarre emotions, physical weakness, diminished internal energy and diverted external energy – I had the lot! Right down to the erratic horizontal lines across the forehead.

I checked to see if my husband had roving eyes. They're the result of Yin nervous tension and invariably mean a fluctuating heart.

It was then I realised it was time to give up our silly Yin existence. 'We're changing our lives with Professor Chee Soo's Ch'ang Ming diet,' I told the family. 'No more poisonous potatoes and tomatoes. From now on it's dates and brown rice and soya beans.'

They stared at me with blank faces.

'But we were on an Adelle Davis high protein diet last week,' the older one said.

'And we were vegetarian Buddhists the week before,' his younger brother added.

'Well, if you don't want to follow the road to truth and live 200 years, that's okay by me,' I said.

'Gee, Mum. Are you really going to live to be 200?'

I chewed thoughtfully on a date. Fifty times.

I saw myself, a sprightly 199, staggering down to the supermarket. The neighbours would wave and say, 'She's so alert – *for her age*.'

There wouldn't be any other old folks to stand around the piano and sing prehistoric Beatles' songs with. Professor Chee Soo and I would be the only ones left. And I'm not sure he even likes the Beatles.

I fingered through coins in my purse. There was just enough to buy hamburgers and chips for everyone.

LIFE CAN BE FATAL

Sometimes I feel like giving up. The wholemeal bread is the consistency of stone, the yoghurt is turning green and my stomach churns the thought of another drink of brewers yeast. Chocolate eclairs, roast dinners and mountains of fresh, steaming white bread coated with real butter come to mind. Then I bite my lip.

It wouldn't do to die at thirty because of an obsession with food that was bad for me. Nobody would have any sympathy.

It's now widely accepted that we must adopt more healthy eating habits. A contact at the French embassy says even the French are giving up their delicious long loaves and croissants for wholemeal bread. Sacre bleu.

The trouble with health food is its advocates are often weedy and sickly-looking. You wonder if they're obsessed with health food because they're unwell. Or did health food make them look like that?

It's no use pondering. Better to work out which rung of the health-food ladder potential friends are on. The easiest way is to get invited for a meal at their place first. If you're unfortunate enough to be cultivating a purist you'll be lucky if your friendship survives the evening.

They believe all food is evil and will offer you a little porridge, water and borage leaves.

Eye their food carefully. Are there more than two salads? Are they sprinkling yeast on their soup? Are they drinking orange juice instead of wine?

If the answer is yes to all these, there's no hope of living down to their standards. When you have them over to your place, you'll find yourself apologising for the food you offer, and never quite know why.

Look for someone who's less hard-core health food.

Someone you won't have to make yoghurt for and, if you do, won't hold it to the light, stir it critically and ask to inspect your culture.

This person will appreciate the fact that you actually managed to grow your own vegetables, without making pointed remarks about inorganic fertilisers.

They have the potential to turn into someone you could relax and eat nuts with. Then, maybe once or twice a year, you could go out together and eat cream donuts.

*

It was a crisp, warm day – rare for our end of Homespun Grove. I bounded outside to stretch in the sun.

'You'll get skin cancer if you stay out there too long,' my husband said.

I put away the suntan oil and went to visit a friend who spends most of her days knitting and talking.

She sat on the edge of her chair and made jittery conversation. Her hands flapped awkwardly. Something was wrong. She wasn't knitting.

'Did you finish the Aran jersey?' I asked.

'No,' she said. 'Didn't you read in the paper the other day that knitting causes bladder cancer?'

First it was artificial colourings, smoking and saccharine we had to give up in order to survive.

It sounded sensible, and it was fun to prove you had a will to live. But each new medical research announcement reveals yet another deadly weapon concealed in our everyday lives. It's getting to the point where our institutions are being nibbled away. A neighbour gives you a glass of beer. Is he trying to poison you or is he plain ignorant? Check if his wife is giving your kids yeast extract sandwiches. It's proof they've got it in for you. Eye those pink fluffy cakes she's handing round so freely. Does she ever eat one herself?

Coffee and tea are nasty, addictive poisons. Sugar is just about criminal.

Don't think you can go all sporty to make up for the bad things you're doing to your body, either. A jog round the block may overstrain your heart or dislocate your breasts. If that doesn't kill you the exhaust fumes will.

I never used to notice exhaust fumes. Now the smell makes me giddy and I can feel the lead sticking to my lungs. A swim in the sea has me so busy peering in the water for pollutants I can't enjoy myself. Swimming pools have me choking with chlorine.

It got to the point where I couldn't stand it any more. I rushed over to see an old yogi friend who does pottery and lives off herbal potions.

'I know exactly what you mean,' he soothed. 'Let me give you a few recipes for natural, health-giving foods. Grind your own flour, do yoga four times a day and you'll live forever. Another cup?'

'Yes, please. That's lovely herbal teal. What's it made of?'

'Comfrey.'

'Comfrey?!' I shrieked. 'Didn't you hear on the news that comfrey causes liver cancer?'

*

Food is a great source of hang-ups.

'An animal Auschwitz' is how my English mother-in-law described our country when she hurtled the length of it in a rental car.

She said we could keep our thermal mud pools. The South Island's lofty peaks were no better than Austria's. Paddocks of penned-in animals waiting for human executioners to deliver the big D were all she saw.

I suppose it's pretty scandalous for a country to make its living out of mass slaughter. She would have felt happier if we survived on something nice and bloodless – like factories.

I could see her point. I winced, recently, trying to describe to our three-year-old how the nice cow in his book metamorphosed into the steaming roll of roast beef below it.

The day a kid learns meat doesn't grow on trees along with everything else is a turning point.

I remember it very well. I didn't eat meat for what seemed like six months. I had lost faith in the unquestionable goodness and rightness of adults. After all, they'd spent most of my life telling me animals were cute and furry. Baa, baa, black sheep and all that. Then it turned out I'd been gobbling the poor wretches the whole time.

How was I to know a family pet wouldn't be next to turn up on my plate? I felt like a blameless participant in an evil regime. Life was a misery. Worse was to come.

I'd stopped eating meat, but the world had not. My parents slobbered over joints of dead animals, oblivious of my cold stares.

Sheep trucks reeking with fear continued to rumble off to the works (how typical of adults to give a place of horror such a harmless name).

I came to regard my farming cousins as enemies concealing murderous natures under veneers of easy-going cheerfulness.

Then the crisis came. Fish was for tea.

'Come on now,' Mum coaxed. 'Fish can't feel as much as other animals. They don't have as many nerve endings.'

This was another adult lie in the murder department, I decided. Plumes of steam rose from the milky flesh. My nostrils tingled with the delicate aroma. It looked as if fish blood might not even be red.

I hadn't considered degrees of agony before. Perhaps Mum was right and people should limit compassion according to the density of nerve endings. Had anyone heard a beetroot scream as it was wrenched from the ground?

My plate was scraped clean of fish and its sauce before the argument could be completed.

The following night it was easier to eat part of a cow – considering I'd already devoured a fish in cold blood.

*

If people are snobbish about food, they're ten times worse about wine.

The air was heady with the scent of honeysuckle. Hot wind came in a steady stream – as if God had left his fan heater on.

Our little group stretched out on the grass and mutilated sandwiches. Picturesque? Perhaps.

Our friend Eric rummaged in his car's boot and strode back with two plastic carry bags. 'Got it!' he called, pink with pleasure.

He flourished a tea towel and polished six already sparkling glasses. 'Just wait till you taste this,' he chattered, trying to suppress his excitement. 'An introspective red with notes of lavender and babies' armpits.'

The cork seemed to heave a sigh of relief when Eric eventually prised it out of the bottle. 'Better let it breathe,' he announced.

I peered into the neck to see if the wine was gasping for air.

It's times like this I yearn for the days when my student friends guzzled beer from bottles disguised in brown paper bags. The cops were always on the lookout for excuses to arrest us, and they found drinking in a public place was a good one. We drank beer surreptitiously behind communal toilets and, on more formal occasions, under picnic rugs. Back in those days, a plastic mug was considered pretentious.

Wine drinking is a cult in adolescence. For a while, it was classy to take a bottle when you were invited to dinner. If you took a quality drop, it would disappear quickly into the host's kitchen cupboard while he served the vitriolic junk he'd bought on special.

On the other hand, if you took cheap stuff you'd be forced to drink your own poison.

Then, strangely, classy people stopped taking wine to dinner parties. They brought flowers or chocolate, or a mysterious gadget for peeling garlic. The rest of us were left floundering.

A French family, new to Homespun Grove, came over for a barbecue recently.

'Can I tempt you to a South Island sauvignon?' my husband asked.

Jacques raised our bottle of local nectar and studied the label.

'Beer, please,' he said in a tone etched with pity.

Then Jacques invited us for the inevitable sip of French wine at their place. I carefully put the crystal glass at my feet.

'What a beautiful oriental carpet!' I exclaimed. As my foot shot out to admire the pattern, my wine glass skittered across the rug.

We watched aghast as the red wine formed rivulets of blood before sinking deep into the weave.

None of it would've happened if they'd given me beer in a plastic mug.

'That'll do!' Eric's voice jolted me into the present. He tilted the bottle. Wine danced obediently into the six glasses. I raised mine to my lips.

'Wait!' he yelled.

I froze. Was there a spider in my drink?

'You can't just swill it!! Aerate your mouth first.'

'But I've done that already,' I moaned. 'It was open for at least three seconds.'

He jerked the liquid to the back of his throat and started a series of oral gymnastics that could be described as gargling.

'Got to get it to every part of your tongue,' he gurgled.

I looked down at my glass. Truth to tell, I was hanging out for a beer.

SAFER TO STAY AT HOME

We called it the Murder House. Its pastel-coloured weatherboards and white net curtains concealed the horror that went on inside. It emanated a clean, evil smell that can still turn my stomach to stone.

The dental clinic was tucked away in a corner beside the school gates. Nobody willingly went near the place. We ran past it on the way home. There was no telling when the resident ogress might come out and claim one of us. Or she might spot you through her net curtains and remember it had been a while since she'd prised your jaw open.

The dental nurse wore a stiff white uniform that was more an outer shell than a dress. She was Dracula's massive bride, complete with white stockings, white shoes and nonsensical veil. Everything about her was on a massive scale. I dreaded being clasped to her starchy bosom while she scratched at my teeth with her fearsome instruments.

Some said she wasn't a real dental nurse, but an evil woman who was practising on children till she knew how to do it. Others said she collected children's fingers to take home and roast on Sundays.

We all dreaded the day our number came up. A child, pink-faced and swollen, would stumble fresh from the ordeal into the classroom, and announce, 'Helen Blackman has to go to the dental clinic.'

Our teacher was unusually sensitive about that: 'Don't say Helen *has* to go to the clinic. She doesn't *have* to go. You say, "Could Helen Blackman please go to the dental clinic?"' I had to go anyway.

My insides turned to lead as I climbed the steps to the dental nurse's lair. If the door to her surgery was shut it was a signal to sit on a bench in the foyer and listen to the sound of her drilling some other poor kid's mouth out.

Perched on that miserable bench, I learnt to bargain with God. If I promised to never eat another lolly could He please make the dental nurse give me the all clear this time? God always seemed to be on another line.

As her door creaked open, my heart would pound in my ears. With the resignation of a French countess mounting the scaffold, I'd crawl into the chair. The nurse would then encase me in a giant paper apron.

Paralysed, I'd watch her puddle inexpertly with silvery prods the size of swords, hooked instruments large enough to hang a sheep on. If things went badly – as they usually did – she produced her ultimate weapon, the drill.

Dad reckoned I was lucky to have an electric drill. When he was a boy, the dentist propelled his drill by pumping his foot up and down on a pedal. Dad could also remember when his local fire brigade consisted of four horses and men with brightly polished brass hats.

One of the many goals parents set themselves is to protect their offspring from the traumas they went through. Ours was a generation of terrible teeth, as were generations before us. Maybe better healthcare, improved technology and a richer understanding of child psychology will free our kids from dentistry phobia.

Nevertheless, I delayed taking him to the dental nurse for as long as possible, until I ran out of excuses. I clutched his soft little hand and burst into the surgery. The nurse was young and cheerful. Her uniform was the same as in the old days but her bosom was quite small.

He sat obediently in her chair while she investigated his mouth.

'What lovely teeth you have!' she said. 'Spit in the bowl and I'll give your teeth a tickly polish. Look at my pretty orange toothpaste.'

It was over quickly. It was nothing like the horror I remembered. 'How was it?' I asked as we walked hand in hand back to the car.

'Murder,' he said.

*

While one kid was having his teeth examined, the other was doing his best to get his knocked out. Despite my attempts to interest him in violin lessons, our six-year-old was determined to play rugby.

First was the weigh-in.

'It's not fair,' he said. 'They're putting all the smallest guys in my team. How are we going to beat those big guys?'

I tried to explain they'd bring a team of little guys from another part of town to play his lot. They'd all be the same size.

Then came the game. I dressed incognito so none of my pacifist friends would see me heading for the rugby field. Wind blasted the grounds. My blood seemed to drain to my feet, where it froze solid.

The whistle blew and my kid's team burst into furious attack – on each other.

The coach desperately separated them and faced them in the direction of the team in blue jerseys. The game crawled into action.

'Come on, blue!' a hysterical dad shouted next to me. 'Get stuck in there!'

I tried to think of something suitably vicious to scream at our team, but the sight of delicate six-year-old limbs left me without inspiration. They looked like young chickens scuttling over a farmyard. They were too far away to hear, anyway.

I was relieved to see my kid was wise enough to avoid getting hold of the ball. He stayed pretty much in the background, dishing out sly punches and kicks to blue team players.

'It's no more violent than what they do in school playgrounds,' another mother said.

It seemed healthy exercise – especially for those who stayed out of the action. Coaches probably suffered most – from mental anguish. But they were good-natured about their teams' erratic behaviour.

At half time, the players scrambled for oranges. Kids who never touched the ball during the game took it aside to fondle it and see what it felt like.

The whistle blew, the boys took their positions and – curses! Someone had swapped the goals around.

'Run the other way!' the blue team dad bellowed.

The ball-carrier charged on regardless and scored a perfect try at the wrong end.

Blue lost, so we went home happy. I seized the car trip as an opportunity for a lecture.

'If you're rough on the rugby field you must be gentle at other times,' I said. 'It's important to be gentle and you *are* a gentle person, aren't you? Maybe we could look into violin lessons for next term.'

'Yeah,' he said. 'Who are we fighting next week?'

*

The circus is for kids. Well, I didn't want older boy to miss out on anything. His brother was too young, so it was just the two of us.

A giant green mushroom sprang up on the raceway overnight. We joined the crowd streaming to it like pilgrims. It was a full house, and our seats were on a plank in the back row beside the artists' exit. The ring seemed miles away and I hoped the performers would swivel around to face us from time to time. Still, it was exhilarating sitting in a sea of people waiting for something big to happen – and we did have an excellent view of the band.

'I want something to eat.'

It didn't seem fair to deprive him. All the other kids were slurping and chomping. I bought a box of lollies.

The band struck up and filled my eyes with tears. Pathetic, but brass bands always make me cry. This mawkish tendency probably means I have the potential to become a dictator of a European nation. A kaleidoscope of lavish costumes soon transported me to a world of tacky glamour.

I laughed at the clowns, marvelled at the trapeze artists, and held my breath for the lion tamer. Bodies I could never imagine growing old worked just as well upside down.

Maybe it was a second-rate circus, but things seemed to go wrong more often than expected. When the pony rider fell off her horse, she climbed back on and started again. I perspired for her.

Some performers were gutsy beyond belief. How could a woman who dropped bottles when she was juggling have the nerve to climb to the top of the tent with swords in her mouth?

A lifetime of foot juggling can do strange things to your shape. Bodies that'd seemed perfectly proportioned when they were upside down in the ring appeared slightly malformed as they strode towards us and the exit.

Performers' faces were strained with exertion as they left the tent.

The lion tamer seemed elated. The woman who'd fallen off her horse was on the brink of tears. It seemed unfair the audience had forgotten them already.

I glanced at our son to gloat on the magic in his eyes. But he was bent over his knees, and with great concentration, aiming a string of saliva at a crack in the floor. The tightrope walker edged along his wire. I caught my breath.

'I'm hot,' the kid said. 'I want to go home.'

'Look at the man. Isn't he clever? Don't you wish you could do that?'

'No.'

The trapeze artist swished through the air, slipped and fell into the net. The audience gasped in a single breath. I clutched the plank.

'Hey! Look what I found,' the voice beside me said. I tore my eyes from the ring.

'Chewing gum,' he said, chewing contentedly. 'It was stuck under the seat.'

I made him eject it into my hand – a lump of horrible grey stuff bequeathed by some equally bored kid some days or weeks earlier.

He glowered and whined about going home again.

I bribed him with Coke and let the glittering action carry me away on a cloud.

An hour later, he shot out of the tent without a backward glance.

'Come on!' he said. 'Let's get home before *Batman* finishes on TV.'

*

Houses glowed in sunlight, the air was sweet with blossom smells.

There was only one place to go on such a perfect day.

We struggled through the mesh door, pushchair and all.

'The train!' the six year-old yelled. 'I want to go on the train.'

'We'll see.' The dull ache in my back reminded me the zoo was not designed for pushchairs. I examined the map on a board beside the gate, selected the path that involved the least number of steps and trudged up the slope.

But the tigers caught our older son's eye. He dragged us off my designated route and down a flight of steps. The big cats were muscular and magnificent. Their musky smell tickled our nostrils.

I propped the pushchair up so Three-year-old could see over the concrete wall and through the bars. Stripes inside bars were practically camouflage.

I lowered the pushchair and reached for Six-year-old's hand. But he was already a small figure in the distance, running towards a crowd gathered around a ticket booth. The elephant with her ancient cracked skin was taking people for rides. The zookeeper led her with a hook round the trunk. Once round the empty ornamental pond, and they stopped for a change of passengers.

A cluster of passengers perched incongruously on her saddle. They stared down from the blue sky. Elephant high is pretty high.

'Please, *please,* can I have a ride on the elephant?'

'No, not today. You're too small to go up there on your own.'

'No I'm not. *Please!*'

'All right. You can choose. Either you have a ride on the elephant or a ride on the train. Okay?' A masterpiece of parental cool-headedness.

'Elephant! Elephant!'

Seeing him up there I felt helpless. What if the hook caught a nerve in the elephant's trunk and she suddenly went berserk? The zookeeper would be the first victim trampled by her stumpy feet, unless he was incredibly nimble. She'd hurl children all over the place as she lolloped down the hill. Motherhood had taught me to imagine catastrophes.

I almost wept with relief when Six-year-old strolled towards me brandishing a card from a professional photographer.

For a few moments he was deeply satisfied. Then they saw the toffee apples. Three-year-old slurped his all over his face and jacket. I tried to dab him clean with the hem of my skirt, but he was a tar baby.

Conversation waned as they crunched away. I seized the opportunity for a lecture.

'Do you know what that animal's called?' I asked.

'Nope.' (Crunch.)'It's an ostrich.'

'Emu,' a voice snapped from behind.

I peered out the corner of my eye to see a grey-haired woman in a vinyl coat. Heat crept up my neck.

'Er. It's an emu,' I said humbly.

But he was down at the rabbits already.

Next was an empty pen with a sign 'Ostrich' on the wire. I looked at it sadly. The emu walked through a gate in his pen and stood proudly behind the ostrich sign. A bird of true compassion.

The kiwi house had a sign outside: 'No pushchairs'. I heaved Three-year-old into my arms and fumbled down the dark passage. Once our eyes adjusted, shapes began to appear.

As we watched a kiwi plod up and down behind the glass I couldn't help smiling. God must've been in a whimsical mood when he bestowed upon a flightless brown chicken with a comically long beak.

A possum stared expressionlessly at us through the dark red light. 'Look, a possum,' Six-year-old said.

'Yes,' I replied approvingly. 'I'm not sure what this animal is over here. It looks a bit like a possum but I don't think it is.'

The snappy voice caught me by surprise. 'Wrong again,' it said. 'That IS a possum.'

Through the darkness I could discern the outlines of a vinyl coat.

It was time to go home. I tried to say no, but weakness or exhaustion took over. Before I knew it, we were squeezed into a passenger carriage jiggering round the lake in the train.

Six-year-old grinned up at me victoriously. I'd lucked out on the Firmest and Fairest Mother Award again.

THE NAKED TRUTH

'What a dear little boy,' the lady in the swanky underwear shop said.

I felt a glow of pride as I admired her rows of luscious undies.

She watched with snake eyes as I placed my hand on an appropriately subdued pair of blue knickers.

'How about this style?' she said, holding up a froth of red and black lace.

'No, actually I prefer panties with crotches.'

The kid began sniffing ostentatiously. The shop lady threw herself protectively against her wares.

'Here, have a hanky,' I muttered.

'But this place smells,' he said accusingly. The lady stiffened.

'Yes, it smells lovely, doesn't it?' I said quickly. 'Like perfume …'

'It smells *horrible*!' he said, fingering a lacy bra. 'Is this her old stuff?'

The shop assistant looked ready to throttle him with the nearest suspender belt. I snatched the bra out of the child's hands and swept him out the door.

We crossed the road to the bank where he seized a fistful of glossy brochures off a low glass tabletop. I tried to prise them out of his hand. He went purple and was about to raise hell. It was a choice between a public screaming match with him, or enduring poisonous looks from other customers.

I settled for the glowers and let him keep the brochures while

I waited in line to deal with the teller. We were loyal customers, after all. A few minutes later, an elderly man smiled and waved goodbye as we headed for the exit.

'Got a klepto in the family?' he called after us.

The pizza shop looked safe. Nothing to pinch. Nobody to offend. We made our order, stepped back from the counter and waited. An enormous man waddled into the shop.

'The usual?' the waitress asked.

'Yep. One large pizza with everything.'

I wasn't on guard. My mind was elsewhere, wondering if the asterisk on the calendar meant my period was late. Either that or the dog was due for worming. I used to put ticks in red ink for the days my period was due until the six-year-old stole my pen and ticked every day in red ink.

'Look at his *fat*!' the voice beside me shouted.

'What?'

'That man,' said the child in awed tones. 'How did he get so *fat*??!' The man's face turned redder than the tick on my calendar.

'Ouch! Why did you kick me, Mum?'

'I didn't.'

'Yes you did!'

I made a mental note to hire a babysitter for the next decade or so.

*

Among my many psychotic conditions is shop assistant phobia. It started around the time it became fashionable for bored, rich women to take up little part-time jobs in boutiques.

These women are dangerous, their motives mysterious and terrifying. Chances are they have degrees as long as a broken night. Their wit is gorse-prickle sharp, their taste flawless. They lurk behind potted palms waiting to pounce and emotionally destroy people like me.

My biorhythms have to be at their peak before I can summon enough courage to step through their polished glass doors.

Lord knows what I was thinking wanting brandy glasses. They were hardly going to whisk me out of Homespun Grove to Nirvana. Come to think of it, there was a Nirvana Court down the hill from us. I didn't want to live there, either. The cut crystal glasses winked at me through a shop window and lured me inside. Bulbous and sparkling, the most beautiful brandy glasses glittered from the top shelf. I raised a hand to touch one.

'Can I help you?' she crooned. It wasn't an ordinary 'Can I help you?' The words came like violin notes. Clear, direct, in tune. Her face was refined, if a little severe. This woman had lived. Two husbands and a successful menopause, perhaps. Whatever, she had no need for assertiveness classes.

'I was just looking.' My voice sounded child-like, as I withdrew my hand. 'They are beautiful.'

'Yes, but these are better,' she said, producing two plain looking specimens from the bottom shelf.

'I rather like the shape of the ones up there,' I said, meaning I was attracted to their glitz.

'These are much more a brandy glass shape,' she said. 'The ones you like look like overblown wine glasses. And they're rather gauche.'

I looked wistfully up at them. How could I possibly confess I preferred gauche?

'Just a minute.' She swooped one of the gauche glasses off the shelf and held it up alongside one of her 'better' ones.

'Julia, dear!' she called to the assistant who was up to her nose in bone china. 'Which of these brandy glasses do you prefer?'

'Oh, the one in your left hand. I have some like that at home. The other isn't quite so …'

I sensed a plot and checked the stickers on the bottoms of the glasses. The ones they wanted me to buy were actually cheaper than the ones I wanted. They thought I should stay in the plain brandy glass class where I belonged.

'I'm sure you'll be pleased with these,' she said as she swathed her brandy glasses in tissue paper and handed them to me.

At home, they jostle for position with the Woolworths glasses on the shelf above the fridge. I have to admit brandy does taste better out of them.

But I can't help wondering how brandy would've tasted from the glasses I *really* liked. Rather gauche, probably.

*

The handbag must have been invented pretty soon after the fig leaf. I can't imagine Eve getting by without one for long.

I once saw a photo taken at an American nudist colony. Amongst all the breasts and buttocks stood a naked sylph wearing a shoulder bag.

Perhaps it's a psychological need. One expert said women yearn for freezers because of a twisted maternal drive. Maybe it's the same with handbags. The shoulder strap is the umbilical cord that's never severed. That said, I've yet to be caught breathing heavily over a freezer or a handbag.

The handbag is indispensable because noone has pockets that big.

My old handbag hadn't been the same since I'd carried someone's pet mouse around in it. I felt a pang of sadness as I examined its tired contours for the last time.

The lining was stained with pink streaks from last summer when a lipstick had melted. There was a lingering sickly smell from the time a yoghurt pot exploded. Or was that a mousey smell? Nothing could get rid of the teeth marks on the bottom right-hand corner where the dog had chewed it.

I buried it respectfully in the rubbish tin and went to the handbag shop.

'A woman's handbag should match her size,' the matronly bag lady said, slapping a voluminous backpack on the counter. 'This would suit you.'

Rows of handbags shone from the shelf behind her, each waiting to be bought and abused. Most of them had no potential. I needed one that looked reasonably scruffy from the start so I wouldn't feel disappointed when it fell to pieces.

'How about this?' she said, putting the backpack away. 'I call this a French Connection bag.'

It looked like the sort of thing Audrey Hepburn might wear with alligator shoes.

'Marvellous bags in that film *The French Connection*,' she went on. 'One of the stars had a handbag exactly like this. I went three times just to look at the handbags.'

My memories of the film consisted of cars screeching down endless streets and a gush of relief after I escaped the cinema.

'Go on,' she said, thrusting the bag at me. 'Just hold on to it a while.'

I took the bag and looked in the mirror.

The bag was obviously a chameleon. In my hands it no longer whispered hints of Parisienne romance. It looked like a container for bowling balls and a track suit.

'Perfect,' the bag lady said.

'It looks a bit sporty …'

'Nonsense. All you have to do is buy a pair of decent shoes, a silk scarf, dye your hair, wear more make-up …'

'Have you anything else?'

She gazed fondly at the bag. 'I'm thinking of buying that one for myself,' she sighed. The woman was in love with the thing. After that lecture about tidying myself up, I was beginning to like her less. The thought of depriving her became tantalising.

'I'll take it.'

Another customer came in as I wrote the cheque. I paused before I went to the door. The bag lady was pushing a wine-coloured vinyl sack at her new victim. 'I call this a French Connection bag …'

*

'Excuse me. Your little boy's got no clothes on.'

We were at the local pool and I was struggling to put swimming trunks on a squirming child. The other had run off during changing proceedings.

I hadn't planned to shock the world with a naked three-year-old.

I squinted into the sun and looked up at the offended face. It belonged to a fortyish, middle executive type. He carried an air that implied he was intimate with success. The silly towelling cap suggested an overdose of self-confidence.

Though offended by a naked three-year-old, he was the type who wouldn't mind a few naked women stashed away in a magazine in a dark corner of his desk.

I grabbed the child, wrapped a towel around his waist and squeezed him into his swimwear.

I forgot about nudity hang-ups for a while after that. It wasn't till we rented a cottage in a warmer part of the country that the question came up again.

Our landlady was an older woman with an extensive collection of toby jugs. Her husband, Graham, with his deeply lined face, prominent nose and yellowing teeth, could've been mistaken for being part of her collection.

'I'd better warn you, there's a nudist beach on the other side of the rocks,' she said. 'We never go near them. They're strange people.'

A meat-axe and a belt of bullets were on display on their kitchen wall. Well, you never know when a bunch of nudists might go on a violent rampage.

That afternoon, we sat on the deserted 'clothed' beach while droves of people plodded past. The sand was soon ploughed up with their footprints heading for the rocks.

When a troop of Boy Scouts marched past, I couldn't resist any longer.

We gathered up the kids and joined the scramble over the rocks. As we climbed down the other side, we met the flustered scoutmaster, who was pointing out the fascinations of a cave in the cliff. His group of boys was far more interested in the naked female bather crouching anxiously in the shallows.

Once the scoutmaster had mustered his troop and escorted them back to the clothed beach, the woman rose from the water and strolled to shore. She was wearing a sunhat. Her breasts were swinging like a pair of half empty sacks. Though tanned all over, hers was a lived-in body with rolls, stretch marks and cellulite. She joined a giant walrus of a man who was asleep face down on a towel.

The nudists, mostly men, sunbathed alone or in pairs away from the shoreline near the sand dunes. Most of them were overweight, the wrong side of fifty and a reminder of why clothes were invented.

The other men were too beautiful to be straight. Those who (judging by their dark tans) were hardened nudists, expressed their individuality with stylish sandals, expensive-looking sunglasses or designer hats.

The only people who seemed to feel awkward about being on the nude beach were fullly dressed pervs like us. My husband took a sudden interest in the rock formations and the colour of the sea while our boys swam happily with the unclothed.

We soon noticed the nude beach was blessed with softer sand than we had outside the holiday cottage. The water was clearer and less affected by the tides.

As the week wore on, we gave up resisting and joined the daily pilgrimage to the other side of the rocks. Without swimwear, my body slipped through the water. I felt free and, like a mythical creature, at one with the sea.

Diving through a wave one afternoon, I came face to face with a whale of a man. As he shook his head and sent droplets of water arcing through the air, I felt a shudder of recognition. It was Graham, our landlady's living toby jug, who hated nudists. He was naked as the day.

SOME HOPELESS MORON

Mum believed it was universally acknowledged that a dairy farmer in possession of a good fortune must be in want of a wife. Sadly, our farming cousins and their friends were nothing like Mr Darcy. Their hands were calloused, their conversation minimal and most of them carried a lingering aroma of cow shit.

Nevertheless, Mum insisted we take them seriously because they were much richer than us. Besides, she was probably doing her best to stop my sister and me fantasising about sailors.

I couldn't imagine spending the rest of my life sloshing about in mud milking cows twice a day, but I was willing to at least make an effort to help Mum fulfil her dream for me.

Hoping we might snare a pair of rural gents, she encouraged my sister to take me along to a Saturday night dance at the Queens Hall. Mum pulled out her sewing machine and ran up a powder blue princess line dress for the occasion.

I slipped into my slingback shoes with the pointy toes and looked in the mirror. Something was missing. False eyelashes. I put them on as straight as possible and added a streak of Revlon's latest peel-off eyeliner. Shiny, it was, like licorice. For the finishing touch, I reached for a bottle of the female equivalent of Old Spice – a chokingly powerful perfume called Intimate.

With it being my first non-school dance, I was expecting something incredibly sophisticated. But the Queens Hall turned out to be a corrugated iron shed. We arrived at eight to stare at an empty dance floor. It gave us plenty of time to size up the band. The Nevadas were world famous in our town. Disappointingly, the lead singer wore a wedding ring. Still, his rendition of 'Proud Mary' was so good a few girls got up and danced with each other. The girl couples were invisible to most of us, because nobody had heard of lesbianism in our town.

My sister told me the blokes always showed up after the pubs had closed. Sure enough, just after 10 p.m., a cluster of silhouettes appeared at a doorway in the corner. They stood there, exuding testosterone while we girls sat meekly on benches around the hall's perimeter. We must've looked like a herd of cows waiting for milking.

As the singer launched into 'Quando Quando', a couple of blokes broke away from the bunch and asked girls to dance. I prayed someone would ask me. A ruddy-faced guy with large thighs plodded towards us. I stood up, but he reached across me and grabbed my sister's hand.

Watching them glide onto the floor, I wondered what was wrong with me.

Did I look too young? Was one of my eyelashes falling off?

As the girls peeled away one after the other into masculine arms, I began to realise I was practically the only one who hadn't been claimed. I didn't care. It didn't matter. I was only there to have fun. Except I wasn't.

Then, in the shadows across the hall something moved. A youth whom nature had endowed with neither looks nor confidence made a slow and painful path towards me.

Eye contact would've been fatal. It would've guaranteed he would've asked the other reject girl standing behind me, or made for the loo. They were always going to the loo. With a mounting sense of dread, I knew this scavenger of the dance floor was ugly, sweaty and pimply enough to … 'Err, wanna … dance?'

And short! AND bad breath!!

Mum said it was cruel to turn blokes down because underneath it all they had Delicate Egos. The boy and I crawled across the floor like a couple of crayfish.

His hands were soft and smooth, so he wasn't a farmer. Though Mum would've been disappointed, I was quietly relieved. I'd seen what farmers got up to in their spare time. A couple of cousins had driven us over a paddock once to show us how to slit a sheep's throat.

When he asked how old I was I upped my age by a couple of years. In return, I asked him what he did. Funeral director, he replied.

Being committed to an absent sailor boyfriend had advantages. After the dance, when the funeral director drove me up Churchill Heights and wanted me to do more than admire the view, I had a perfect excuse to put an end to the sweatiness and heavy breathing. I was Waiting for Someone.

*

I never learnt to flirt. Fear of flirting is one of the reasons I rushed into marriage. Safely tucked away in Homespun Grove, there's nothing to flirt with apart from the sausages inside the fridge. But I have a friend who's an expert.

Put a man within six feet of her and she lights up like a shop window. Her eyes glow like a pair of neon full stops and her skin becomes tinged with sunset colours. She spreads her lips to expose rows of unbelievably white, even teeth. Her voice takes on the texture of creme de cacao. She can make 'How are you?' sound like an invitation into the nearest empty storeroom.

Within seconds, her victim's ears turn red and he starts dropping things. Some men try to keep up with her enticing banter. They end up wallowing in a puddle of clumsy innuendo, not knowing if they should apologise or make a bolt for it.

Others charge at her like stallions – only to find they don't understand the delicacies of her craft. They retaliate with bitter and sometimes threatening remarks.

Men may still think they can outshine women in most fields, but few of them understand the subtlety of flirting. Those who *think* they do have no idea how creepy they are. The male flirt teeters in the hinterland of sliminess. His boyish eyes twinkle as he tries to drown women in his charm.

Lately, my friend has been morose. She thinks the flirting tide is turning against her.

'It's all or nothing these days,' she said sadly. 'You don't just go out for dinner with a man. You don't *just* go to a movie. If you're out in public with someone, you're in for the whole deal. What happened to goodnight kisses on the back doorstep?'

'Come to think of it, you don't see couples grappling in cars any more either,' I said.

'If you gaze at stars people think you go to astronomy classes. They ask how long you've been on a diet if you're off your food. There's no thrill of the chase.'

I tried to explain people are realistic about physical functions these days. This way no one's exploited. We can get the whole sex business over and done with and concentrate on the important things in life – jogging, health food and platonic relationships based on mutual respect.

'I must be a dinosaur,' she said, sipping her coffee dolefully.

Even a passing waiter failed to light her eye.

*

Fashionable people are late, so I'm always early.

The host's jaw drops when he opens his front door in his underwear. 'Oh. I thought you were delivering the beer,' he stammers. 'You're ...'

'Early? Sorry. I'll drive round the block.'

'No, no,' he insists. 'Come in. Have a drink.'

I know he doesn't want me to accept, but I honestly have nothing better to do.

It's awkward sitting in a corner of their living room while the hostess drags their dachshund out of the cheese dip and screams at her kids to go to bed.

An hour later, I'm pleasantly weary as people start to trickle in. Two hours on, the party hots up and I can hardly keep my eyes open. I never see the highlights people talk about for weeks afterwards. That stuff happens when I'm back home tucked up in bed.

Early at concerts, I tire of counting the number of times the fire curtain goes up and down. My knees get sore when twenty people squeeze past saying 'S'cuse me'.

My one consolation is I married someone with the same affliction.

We both turned up half an hour early for our wedding. The registry office was particularly busy that day. We sat through two weddings before our own. The couples seemed uneasy with another bride and groom sitting at the back of the hall watching them, but there wasn't much else we could do.

Our shared affliction means we can have meaningful conversations like – 'You're late.'

'No I'm not. I'm on time.'

'Let's see.' (Looks at watch.) 'So you are. You're actually early.'

There's no point setting the alarm clock. We just lie awake and wait for the thing to ring.

Cakes that are supposed to stay in the oven for forty minutes I take out after thirty. Then I wonder why they sink in the middle and taste like scrambled eggs.

The family's used to them but my value as a playgroup mum is about minus three. My soggy cakes always lie sad and unwanted at fundraising stalls.

'Who brought that mess?' someone says.

'Some hopeless moron,' I mutter. 'I might as well buy it and get it out of the way.'

We always find reasons to celebrate birthdays a day or two early.

It doesn't take the tang out of the real day because there's usually something else to do early by then.

*

Office parties are something to avoid going to early or late.

I've not been lucky enough to attend the sort of office do where Mr Smith from accounts drops his trousers on top of the buffet table.

Ours are staid affairs where people dredge up respectable conversation.

'Weren't you pregnant at last year's party?' Barbara Whatsername said, running seagull eyes over my body.

'No, I've been on a diet.'

Party chitchat reminds me of so-called conversations Mum and Dad used to have with our cousins when they came to town. After a cavernous silence, one of the farmers would clear his throat and say, 'How's the gas, Bill?'

I couldn't work out if they were referring to the state of his digestion or the extent of our gas usage. What they really want to hear about was the terrible state of the gasworks and Dad's crackpot schemes for natural gas.

Back at the office party the air was heavy with the smell of beer, cigarette smoke and deodorant. A dispirited band played ten-year-old pop songs too slow for dancing to. Married couples shuffled round the floor, muttering things as their eyes darted round the room.

Gloria's husband from HR asked me to dance. I said yes, and immediately felt naughty.

A group in the corner became determinedly drunk. They probably had the right idea but it was difficult to intrude icy sober. Their talk became louder and slower as the night wore on. Their wives smiled a lot and eyed each other's dresses.

Barbara was in the thick of it, her thoughts as clear as a teleprinter readout: *Is she really wearing the same as last year? She couldn't – wouldn't ... We all know what Gail's up to with her plunging neckline and side splits ... Where's Gordon? ... Oh, there he is, chatting up Mr*

T. from the executive floor … Mr T. looks hypertensive. Overweight too … Wonder who's next in line? …

Hovering beside the drinks table and looking lost, was someone best avoided. I'd been stuck with him the whole evening last year. He'd droned on about the swimming pool he was building in his back yard. In our climate, a pool would be usable maybe six days a year.

When he saw me, his face brightened. I darted behind a small group, but it was too late.

After listening to a detailed account of the challenges of keeping pool chemicals perfectly balanced, I made for the ultimate refuge, The Ladies.

As I rearranged my lipstick in front of the mirror, I could hear the strains of 'Auld Lang Syne'. Even the band wanted to go home.

Couples scattered gratefully for their cars. Only heavy drinkers held rowdy fort at their tables.

'Who is that boring man who makes his own swimming pools?' I asked a pleasant face as we headed for the door.

'My husband,' she replied.

We all said we must do this more often. But in the soundproof shells of our cars I'm willing to bet we were all saying the same thing:

'Thank God that's over.'

*

My son wanted to have his birthday party at a hamburger joint. I wouldn't hear of it. I wanted him to enjoy the magic of the old paper hats and birthday candles routine – with home-made cake.

A plain square or round cake with chocolate icing is extinct. Kids assume their mothers' culinary talents are boundless. They demand train cakes, merry-go-round cakes or three-rabbits-in-bed cakes.

Sweat blistered on my brow as I made finishing touches to what I thought was a superb aeroplane cake.

'My friends won't like that,' the birthday boy said. 'The icing's the wrong colour.'

My thunderous reaction had him scooting out the door.

'My friends *will* like it,' he assured me later. 'They can decide if it's a plane or a castle.'

On the day, other mothers examined my masterpiece with respect. One of them said she'd always wanted to make a boat cake like that.

Our son had desperately wanted an army set for his birthday. I'd finally caved in, hardly believing I was the same person who'd refused to buy toy guns for so long. Nothing like parenthood to promote compromise.

Modern kids don't respond well to traditional party games, most of which have Victorian origins and are unfashionably cruel.

Guaranteed to get a roomful of kids howling is 'Pass the Parcel'. They sulk because they didn't get a turn to unwrap a layer of parcel. Then they sob because they didn't win the prize.

This time, I tucked a sweet in each layer and made sure everyone had a turn at opening the parcel. It put them on a wild sugar high, making it necessary to move on to 'Dead Fish'.

Watching them lie still on the floor trying not to twitch or make a sound was my favourite part of the party.

Unfortunately, they refused to play 'Dead Fish' longer than five minutes. I tried to interest them in 'Musical Chairs' but they preferred to raise hell in their own way with me acting as riot squad.

At last, their parents arrived to take them home.

'Robert's had a great time!' I said, loading him up with a party bag and shoving him out the door.

'No, I didn't!' he yelled.

Next year it'll be a hamburger joint.

DAMP GRASS AND CANVAS

These cornflakes are yucky. All the food in this house is yucky. When are we going home?' The articulate three-year-old and his parents had been staying with us for a very long week.

A flood of unhostessly emotions overcame me. I could have cheerfully stuffed the cornflakes up his nose. I was hurt that his parents didn't rush to defend me and my yucky food.

Time has mellowed me since then. Especially since I've had my own preschoolers to inflict as guests upon other people.

It may sound like a sadistic game to the uninitiated. They would say it is far more sensible not to travel at all with children. Of course they're right. They would say if you simply have to get away, why not stay in a motel?

Motels no longer fit family budgets. Washing nappies at motor camps makes you wish you'd stayed at home. House swaps involve complicated negotiations.

Simple economics insist some families must inflict themselves upon others if they are to get a holiday at all. It's probably safer to land only on relatives. At least they may feel they have an obligation to suffer the odd revolting quirk your kids turn up.

They somehow behave so much more badly when they're away. Maybe they're the same as always and I don't notice it so much at home. Perhaps they just have a bubbling holiday feeling which comes out in nerve-shattering ways.

The little darlings may express their free spirits by defecating on the neighbours' lawn, throwing Grandma's china from the top of her kitchen bench, or scratching up Granddad's lovingly planted seeds.

Grandma and Granddad take us on a drive around the hometown to stop the kids wrecking their house.

'It's about time they pulled this town down,' says Six-year-old. 'It's a dump.'

It's 6 a.m. and our three-year-old dived into bed with Grandma. Not surprisingly, she wasn't responsive. So he poured out a stream of language that would make the inhabitants of a brothel blush.

I winced under my sheets, but there was no reaction from Grandma. Had she suddenly become broad-minded and unshockable, or was she deaf? Maybe her thoughts are so innocent the words sounded like something else.

When we dropped in on a kind aunt she recklessly gave them a chocolate bar each. Ten minutes later greasy brown streaks appeared on her living-room wallpaper. My hasty wall scrubbing removed the chocolate stains as well as the wallpaper pattern. I lamely apologised and offered to patch the mess if she had any spare rolls of the same paper. She didn't.

It takes courage and diplomacy to take kids on a holiday visit.

I hope they ask us back.

*

Easter holidays bring back memories of Dad roping our tent and camping gear onto the trailer he borrowed from a friend at the gasworks. It didn't seem a big deal, but it must've taken our parents days of planning – the food and sleeping bags, stretchers and plastic plates to eat off.

Looking back, I was profoundly ungrateful.

Sandwiched between my older sister and brother on the back seat of our Ford Zephyr 6, I started to feel carsick before we reached the corner of our street.

Many of the roads that snaked across the country were unsealed back then. They'd been specifically designed to make children throw up – or at least think about it.

There were always added dramas – a flat tyre or a renegade wheel flying off the trailer. On one occasion, the entire trailer detached itself and rattled back down a hill in clouds of dust.

I used to wonder why our parents bothered with camping when it put them so on edge.

Once we arrived at the camping site, the tent miraculously put itself up – though the process seemed to require a lot of swearing from Dad. Stretchers would be assembled, and after much argument, placed in strategic positions inside the darkened bowels of the tent.

Deck chairs would be assembled while Mum, who would've preferred being centre stage at Sadler's Wells, would trot off in her pearls to the communal kitchen.

Proust had his madeleines, but I have the smell of damp grass and canvas to carry me back to childhood. And the soft drum of water pelting down on the tent. It always rained.

*

Those memories didn't put me off wanting to share the experience with our little boys. Camping is a rite of passage in our part of the world. When their father refused to join us, I didn't take it personally. He's English, so probably lacked the camping gene.

I figured it was simply a matter of being organised – and expecting the worst. After raiding the medicine chest for bandages and a tired-looking tube of antibiotic cream, I rang my friend Sue. A seasoned camper, she claimed sleeping in a tent with kids could actually be relaxing.

'You'll need plastic plates, bowls and mugs,' she said. I cast a panic-stricken eye over the plate cupboard. 'Cutlery, torch, tin opener, toilet paper, teabags and a pot to boil water in.'

'A pot to boil water in?' I echoed. That sounded a little too primitive.

'Camping's sophisticated these days,' she continued brightly. 'You'll be able to boil yourself a cup in the cookhouse.'

I gazed at our electric jug with new-found affection.

Following her instructions, I invested in a set of plastic plates and a pair of jeans to blend in with the camping mums. A few days later, I stacked the car with blankets, mattresses, raincoats, sleeping bags and children.

'Don't forget this, Mum!'

'Oh for heaven's sake. I haven't room for any more junk. Just leave it there, will you?'

'But it's the tent!' I grudgingly stuffed the lumpy bag on the back seat and perched a kid on top of it.

We hurtled into the distance. Already a vision of an electric jug boiling contentedly appeared in the sky above the road.

'There's a traffic cop!' someone shrieked from the back.

Sure enough, he stood by the roadside and raised his hand slightly. What crime had I committed this time? I lifted my foot.

'It's okay,' the kid said. 'He's just picking his nose.'

With relief I saw the kid was right.The three-hour journey was harrowing. I issued increasingly elaborate warnings about what happens to cars with children who wriggle and fight in the back of them.

Hot, sticky and shattered, we rattled into the campsite at last. The kids sprang out of the car and bounded over the grass with the exuberance they usually reserve for 6 a.m. on Sundays.

'Where's the TV?'

'There's no TV in this camp,' I said. 'We're here for the simple life.'

'Yes there is! It's in the rec room.'

How do kids find things out so quickly?

We walked past caravans clustered around utility blocks. Each home on wheels was more sumptuous than the last. The inhabitants peered through tinted glass as they sipped chilled beer. Television aerials angled into the sky. An open door revealed a glimpse of purple shag-pile carpet and a canary in a cage.

Despite the luxury, the atmosphere wasn't festive. Faces wore haunted expressions, as if they were waiting to see if the next caravan to arrive had more gadgets than theirs. They hadn't Got Away From It at All. 'It' had come with them, complete with the canary.

The tent paddock was tucked in a remote corner. It was more what I'd imagined.

A couple from a nearby tent helped me put the thing up. It struggled in the wind like a great, dying beast.

'They're all wife swappers over there, y'know,' the husband said.

'Where?' I asked.

He shrugged towards the utility blocks. 'Caravans.'

At last, I managed to get the kids prostrate inside their sleeping bags in the tent. As I issued gruesome tales about what happens to children who won't sleep in tents, I wondered if *Dr Who* needed any scriptwriters.

As far as camping adventures go, the night was uneventful. Only one pole collapsed. After that, a cheerful gentleman burst through the flaps and insisted we'd got into his tent by mistake. I eventually persuaded him otherwise and directed him towards his.

I drifted to sleep dreaming of a pot on a cookhouse stove sending a plume of steam into the air. I had no energy to wake up properly to struggle over sharp stones in the dark and make the dream reality.

A group of tents in the morning light is like a gathering of personalities. A plain pup tent emitted a wail from a young baby. A large, brown one quivered in the wind and sneezed ostentatiously. A red and blue nylon job oozed pop music. Some were still asleep. I trudged past them on my way to the shower block, teabags tucked in the pocket of my jeans. Damn! I'd left the pot behind.

A middle-aged lady and I exchanged pleasantries as she scrubbed her dentures in the next sink.

'We come here every year,' she smiled toothlessly.

After breakfast, washing dishes in a bucket, I struck up a friendship with a woman called Eve. Her husband was away a lot with work like mine. Like me, she was camping solo with her kids.

We rounded them up and took them to the beach.

'Nice scenery,' I said. 'Hey! Don't go near the river, you kids!'

'Don't throw sand at people!' Eve yelled. 'And, Anna, don't rub that sun cream off your nose!'

'The facilities are good here,' I said. 'Don't poke that dog's eyes out!'

'And the weather's not bad.' Eve stood up. 'Will you kids stop fighting this minute!? Where's the baby?'

'Eating crabs in the rock pool, I think. Oh and look! One of the boys is out too deep.'

I scampered across the sand and dragged him spluttering and indignant out of the sea.

'What I really like about camping,' Eve said, squeezing a splinter from her child's foot, 'is the relaxation.'

'Yes,' I said, slapping a Messerschmitt-sized mosquito that had just landed on my ankle.

'It's nice to relax for a change.'

Next day, the boys came down with chickenpox.

*

Mosquitoes have a thing for me. Given any hot sultry evening, they'll swarm around me and ignore every other human on the balcony. I wouldn't mind donating so much blood to the species if my physical reaction wasn't so dramatic. A single bite swells up like a volcano and itches for days.

Some people call them mozzies, as if there's something cute and loveable about them. To me they are and always will be mosquitoes.

One summer, we rented a cottage by the sea with the idea of injecting romance into our marriage. The owner had talked it up on the phone, so when the car rattled to a halt outside what amounted to a corrugated iron garage I tried to hide my disappointment.

'An army hut!' our older son called from the back seat. 'Yippee! We can play soldiers.'

My husband slid out from behind the driver's seat and wrestled with the giant padlock holding the so-called front door together.

As he pushed the shack's sliding door sideways the boys squeezed past him and ran inside. I could hear them squabbling over who was going to have the top bunk. My heart sank when I stepped into the shadowy interior. Hot and airless, it was even smaller than it'd looked from the outside.

The 'living area' consisted of a small wooden table and two kitchen chairs that had once been Van Gogh yellow. The stove looked as if it hadn't seen action since World War Two. I swept a cobweb from my hair.

Jammed up against the bunks was a lumpy double bed. The boys took turns jumping off the top bunk onto the bed, which emitted squeals of protest.

'Well, this is taking intimacy to a new level,' my husband said, sitting on the edge of the bed.

I thumped the kitchen window that refused to budge and told the boys to play outside. On the wall above the sink was our only source of hot water, an old cylindrical boiler. I hadn't seen one like it in years. As I turned the tap and watched the water level rise, the boys burst through the door.

'We've found a Nazi hangout!' the younger one cried.

They led us outside down a sandy path to the Nazi's asbestos lair. Boughs of jasmine scrambling over the roof had no hope of neutralising the stench.

As I nudged the door open, a shaft of sunlight fell on a toilet seat fitted into a crude wooden bench. The boys covered their mouths and noses as I pointed out the only swastikas in there were spiders. When I explained the true purpose of the Nazi hangout, the boys were shocked and said there was no way they were going to poo in there.

I asked how long they thought they could hold out. The older one said probably a week.

'Where do you think the shower is?' I asked.

'Over there,' my husband said, after a long pause. He was pointing at the sea.

As the sun began to set, we wrestled the boys in their pyjamas and supervised teeth brushing from a bowl of water. After bedtime stories, we tried to settle them in their allocated bunks – the older one on top. But they were too excited planning tomorrow's Nazi ambush to sleep. I tripped over a battalion of plastic soldiers spread across the floor detailing the battle plan.

The room was as hot as the jungle with the door closed, so we left it open. Before long I heard the familiar dreaded drone.

'Mosquitoes!' I groaned. 'I didn't pack any repellant.'

My husband handed me a can of fly spray. For once, I didn't care what it had it in. I doused the place. The bed squawked as I lowered myself on the kapok mattress. I drifted finally to sleep.

Later, a lady vampire flew into my dreams. A can of fly spray appeared miraculously in my hand. I aimed the nozzle at her horrible head and released a jet of poison.

'Hey! Stop that,' my husband croaked drowsily. 'You'll kill me with that stuff!'

With relief and amazement, I found myself sitting bolt upright in bed, pelting the poor man.

Next morning, I couldn't open my left eye. A half-swollen face peered from the splinter that passed as a mirror. Thanks, mosquitoes.

My husband unloaded rods from the back of the car and disappeared with the boys. They returned an hour later with two tiny fish floating upside down in a bucket. The boys insisted I fry them for lunch, but when they saw the wizened creatures glaring accusingly up at them from their plates, they wouldn't take a bite.

The next two days were hazy. I lay on the bed swatting mosquitoes and thrashing about in a fever in between dashing off to Hitler's bunker (the fish, probably).

By the time we got back to Homespun Grove, my face was swollen and both eyes were half closed. I wore sunglasses. A concerned-looking woman at the shopping centre handed me a brochure with a helpline number for battered wives.

THEY'RE ALL INTO SOMETHING

It's hard being a nebula. Especially when everyone else is into something – divorce, homosexuality, open fires ...

Townspeople used to think they'd had a pretty good country outing if they came home with a bucket of blackberries.

Lucky ones found mushrooms, the non-poisonous variety. Others gathered bulrushes from the roadside to decorate the living room.

It was all picturesque and under control.

I realised things were going wrong when I found a spade in the boot of a friend's car.

'What's that for?' I asked.

'Dung.'

'What?'

'Whenever I go for a drive in the country and see horse dung on the road I stop the car, get the spade and scoop the pile into the boot.'

'Don't you think that's taking ecology a bit far?'

'Not at all,' she replied.

Then I noticed the chainsaw.

'A household's most valuable possession,' she explained. 'I traded my vacuum cleaner for it when electricity prices went up.'

'What do you do with it?'

'Hop in the car. I'll show you.'

Branches leant gracefully over the charming country road.

'Aha!' she said like a hunter who'd found the prey. She stamped on the brake and shot around to the back of the car. She reappeared with the chainsaw, clambered up the tree and started ripping off branches.

'Stick 'em in the boot!' she yelled down from her perch when the saw stopped its racket. 'And watch out for farmers.'

I had no choice. The sooner the logs were in the boot the faster the evidence would be hidden. I heaved a huge stump. 'I didn't know you had an open fire,' I shouted.

'Everyone does these days. Don't tell me you haven't got one of those dinky wood-burning heaters?'

'No.'

'How thoughtless can you get?! What do you think you're doing to the world's resources?'

The chainsaw burst into action again. A huge branch crashed down with squeals of woody agony. I sprinted to the other side of the road. A near miss.

'I'll come down and cut that into more manageable pieces,' she said. 'You'd better climb up here and keep a lookout.'

The tree was too high for me. I scrambled onto a gate and scanned the countryside. A small figure trudged briskly over a hill. What was that over his shoulder? A stick? A shotgun?

'Farmer alert!' I called, as I tumbled off the gate.

We stuffed the remaining logs into the car and roared off.

'Can we go home now?' I begged.

'We're so near the beach,' she said. 'I'll just get a sack of driftwood.'

We jolted to a halt. The beach teemed with people who studied the sand with great concentration. They all carried sacks.

She thrust an enormous bag at me.

'Out and at 'em!' she ordered.

The beach was a battleground. A grown-up version of a lolly

scramble. I didn't get near any driftwood.

'I want to go home!' I wailed.

She agreed. Reluctantly.

Countryside zipped past the car window.

'You really ought to get a wood-burning heater,' she said. 'They're so cheap to run.'

'What happens when all the wood runs out?' I asked.

We arrived back at her house. Her husband was excavating what had been the back garden.

'We'll start digging,' he explained. 'For coal.'

*

Conservation isn't the only thing people are into these days, either. They're all doing it. Everywhere I go. Old people, young unmarrieds, even mothers down at playgroup have started doing it.

I tried to pretend it wasn't happening and went for aspirin to the chemist shop where life should be normal. Clinical rows of shampoo bottles made me feel better.

'Can I help you?' It was one of those girls dressed as if she couldn't decide whether she was a dental nurse or Bo Derek. I studied the row of badges running down to her hemline to see if she was a certified aspirin seller.

A sales rep with a suitcase-load of hypochondriac's delight came into the shop. The assistant walked up to him and – oh no – they started doing it too.

People are kissing, cuddling and touching people they hardly know. I don't mean to sound neurotic, but it's making me nervous. Even the post office teller has started licking my stamps.

On Tuesday when I was wheeling my trolley round the supermarket a tentacle-like arm reached around from behind a display and stroked my shoulder. Cold with fear, I jerked my head around. It was the supermarket manager saying they had a special on lima beans.

I wouldn't be surprised if next time the checkout girl dives at me for a full-on pash.

Even the paper boy lingers on the doorstep as if he's expecting physical contact (on second thoughts, he's probably waiting for a tip).

'It's nothing sexual,' says someone I met for the first time last week as she presses parts of her anatomy I didn't know other women had against me. 'It's simply a return to deeper tribal feelings.'

It's hardly worth going to meetings any more. By the time they've finished groping each other, I'm ready to go home.

Not that I've got anything against intimacy. But this latest hug-your-bus-driver craze smells phony. Someone's brought it back from somewhere, along with 'Have a nice day'. No one can say 'Have a nice day' without sounding like a recording.

We Kiwis were born not to touch each other. Probably complex emotions to do with our Plunket nurses.

Look carefully next time you see them at it. The hugger has a determined grimace as he or she counts how long the clinch should continue. Two seconds for a first meeting, four for a second, six for a third and so on.

The huggee looks desperate and turns red from lack of oxygen.

You can't ask a hugger to stop or have a cup of tea instead. Their tribal instincts could be thwarted.

Then there are the hug-mongers who try to get me to embrace their friends, simply because they went to primary school together. It's time to re-evaluate the friendship when they insist a complete stranger thrust his head at my chest and choke me with clouds of dandruff and garlic fumes.

Personally, I'd rather cut back on body language small talk that doesn't improve communication. It's nearly always people I'd rather not be near who squeeze me to their breast with a 'love the world' expression on their face.

On the few occasions I've tried to conform to the fashion it's all gone wrong. Whenever I've attempted physical contact with someone I thought looked touchable, they've frozen, then winced in my embrace.

For me, intimacy is something altogether different. As a preschooler, I used to have afternoon naps with Mum. I would curl up beside her on her bed, rest my head on her stomach and drift off with the world's most comforting squelches sloshing in my ear.

That was body talk.

So, I think everyone should give up this kissing-cuddling rubbish. It's time to start communicating in a way that's truly meaningful.

Let's listen to each other's stomachs.

HELLO WORLD – REMEMBER ME?

Life was passing me by in Homespun Grove. They used to try to break the morale of war prisoners by making them dig out holes only to fill them in again. But a housewife does that every day. Cleaning rooms for people to untidy three minutes later, washing clothes for them to dirty again, cooking meals that end up being flushed through sewers.

A friend returned from a trip with her latest boyfriend. 'Where did you sleep?' I asked.

'On a beach, of course.'

'In a tent?'

She flashed me a tolerant smile. 'Under the stars.'

I know for sure if I tried to sleep under the stars I'd be washed away by a freak storm. It's always different for other people.

'You must have taken a lot of food,' I said.

'No, we ate seaweed, ferns and shellfish of course.'

'Oh,' I said, impressed. 'Would you like another piece of banana cake?'

'No thanks. I don't go for that over-refined stuff.'

I'd never regarded my banana cake as particularly refined. Perhaps it was a compliment.

'Why don't you bring your boyfriend over some time?' I asked.

'I'd like to,' she said. 'But I don't think he'd approve of your lifestyle – television, meat-eating, lounge suite.'

'A very tatty lounge suite,' I said quickly. 'It hasn't been the same since the boys took to it with an axe.'

'We're really into poverty,' she explained.

'You mean the Third World, vegetable co-ops, flatting in the worst part of town?'

'That's luxury compared to how most of the world lives.'

'Why don't you give him a break from all that hardship?' I said. 'Bring him round to babysit one night. Let him have a touch of luxury.'

She shook her head. 'It would be too embarrassing,' she said. 'You're just too out of touch.'

I tried not to be insulted. Still, I didn't like the idea of being out of touch. That's why I was so grateful when *Time* magazine listed what was 'in' and 'out' for the eighties. At last I had something to go by.

In: plain white sheets, grapefruit juice, squash, wood-burning stoves, cotton undies, diaphragms, Oxford shirts and marriage.

Out: living together, disco, blue eyeshadow, the pill, T-shirts, open shirts and crock pots.

I gave plain white sheets a big tick. Well, they're not exactly plain white any more. I wasn't able to afford floral sheets when they came in. Overdrafts have their advantages.

And marriage. We did that because we were too chicken to live together like everyone else.

Grapefruit juice and squash. With a houseful of kids, stuff like that is guzzled before I get it out of the supermarket bag.

I suspect *Time* magazine was referring to that ridiculous, exhausting sport when it mentioned squash. Personally, I relate to the bottled variety.

A wood-burning stove would be a picturesque and impressive way to show everyone we care. But only millionaires can afford them, and they take as much time to maintain as a part-time job.

I asked the doctor about a diaphragm.

'You could have one if you like,' she said. 'But you might get pregnant.'

No thanks.

I went to town to buy some cotton undies.

'Nobody wears those any more,' the lipsticky girl said.

'Oh. Have you got any Oxford shirts then?'

'What's an Oxford shirt?' she asked.

'I don't know. They're big in America.'

'Hang on. I'll ask Graham in the men's department … He doesn't know either.'

Nobody could say I didn't try.

I hid our *Saturday Night Fever* record and tried to give away all the T-shirts people had been giving me lately. (Why, I wondered?) I'd given up the pill years ago because it made me sick – and pregnant.

I drew the line at burning my husband's open-necked shirts. He's oblivious to fashion trends, anyway.

All that remained was the blue eyeshadow. Sky blue, navy blue, sparkly blue. I gathered up every trace I owned and threw it in the bin.

In town later, I picked over half-price cosmetics with a perky eighteen year-old. I watched in awe as she rubbed extravagant preparations into her skin. I admired how she planned to spend time and dollars on her appearance without the slightest pang of guilt. Was I ever like that?

She looked like someone who knew what was 'in'.

'What do you think of this colour?' I asked, turning over one of the cheaper tubes.

'Hopeless.'

'Metallic Green?'

'No,' she laughed. 'People with our colour eyes should wear this.' She produced a tube of red goo.

What was that she'd said? *Our* colour eyes? Had that vivacious young creature associated herself with me to the extent that we had the same colour eyes?

I bought two tubes of Moody Plum, smeared it generously on my lids and ran to join the bus queue.

A punk rocker of dubious gender flashed me a radiant smile. I hurried to the back of the bus. Two Buddhist monks came and sat next to me. I seemed to be attracting unusual company.

At last I got home, confident I would impress my husband with the new, into-the-right-things me.

'Good God!' he said as I came through the door. 'Who punched you?'

*

The Health Department once suggested in an advertising campaign that there were ten easy ways to have a baby. After having two, I don't know one easy way.

I began to notice an increasingly jaded outlook on life, which could only be old age creeping up on me. It would be more practical if the Health Department produced a brochure to help me recognise the symptoms. Then I'd know when to give up and order my cardboard coffin. They could run it along the following lines:

You are probably growing old when:

- the only whistles you hear when you walk down the street are from the northerly wind whipping around buildings
- there is a whole generation of young people coming along bursting with outlandish ideals you gave up long ago
- people you regard as ancient say in a chummy way 'Of course, people *our* age …'
- thirty no longer sounds like an age for retirement
- you try on some brilliant, frivolous garment, and hear shop assistants giggling behind your back
- watching old movies on television, you could swear you saw them in the cinema a year ago
- you use words like 'trendy', 'hippie' and 'way out'
- crow's feet have nothing to do with birds' toes.

*

I stared out the kitchen window at the desolate landscape of Homespun Grove. What had life as a WAM (wife and mother) done for me anyway? As an adolescent, I'd known what life was about. Clearasil, Cat Stevens and flower power. Anyone over twenty was practically in their coffins.

Then WAM shook me out of childhood and bulldozed me into shape. But I still felt seventeen inside, no matter how old I was.

I learnt marriage isn't one long *Love Story* movie. Babies are not television soap advertisements. They have personalities that could pummel a lioness into playdough.

I learnt how to mop instant pudding off the kitchen ceiling. To escape death by centimetres tearing open lethal yoghurt-carton foil.

WAMhood taught me to tuck a tiny tot into bed with 'Don't be silly. There's no such thing as ghosts' – before creeping back to my room to sleep with the light and radio on.

There was the day I went shopping. People seemed to be glancing disapprovingly at the ground. I looked at my feet – horrors! I was still wearing slippers!

Around that time, I visited a friend who went to a psychiatrist every week. 'Whenever I think I'm really going under,' she said, smiling weakly, 'I remember when you brought your little boy round here with one blue and one red sock on. Then I know things aren't that bad for me.'

There had to be more to life than WAMhood. Everyone else seemed to be doing their own thing. Fulfilled and inflicting their impossible personalities on the world.

I opened the aluminium-framed kitchen window.

'Hey, Homespun Grove!' I bellowed at the windswept gorse. 'What about me?'

*

There's this stuff you can get to blot out the black rings under your eyes. Whether it works or not is anyone's guess. The main thing is the reassurance. If you do have black rings, you know you've done your best – nobody else has the right to notice them.

I was smearing this gunk under my eye in the early morning light. It didn't seem to stop them looking red and puffy. Today was important. My first day at work for seven years. Not real work. Just part-time. But in an office. In town.

That may not sound very dazzling. But for seven years I'd listened to other women glamorising that wonderful thing called Work. That great love they'd sacrificed in order to squeeze babies into the world and wash dishes.

Nobody calls babies and dishes Work. It's slave labour. Or nothing-at-all. Or what you do when you're not lining up in the doctor's waiting room for valium.

I'd sat in suburban kitchens countless times while friends remembered the scintillating creatures they used to be before they'd left Work.

'I'd like to get a proper job,' a friend once said, 'but I'd only earn enough money to pay someone to look after the kids. It'd take me more than a year to save enough to buy clothes to wear to Work.'

Was Work so amazing you had to have special clothes?

I grabbed an old purple shirt from the wardrobe (no pre-feminist blouse for me) and checked it for food stains.

I couldn't remember much of my Working days. They seemed to involve a lot of getting out of a warm bed when I least felt like it.

Then one day this job came up. Only an insane woman would turn it down.

After finishing touches to my bagless eyes, I left my husband with a bedful of breakfast-wanting children and headed down Homespun Grove for the bus. (Yes, Cinderella. You shall go to the ball.)

The bus people looked tired and dowdy. None of them behaved as if the ultimate experience was waiting at the office. A schoolgirl fiddled with her pierced ears. A woman whined about her hysterectomy. A fish-faced man stared longingly at girls on the street.

As our harsh morning perfumes and aftershaves mingled I imagined what a horrible experience it would be to be trapped on a desert island in this bus. Was there anyone I could bear to continue the species with?

On the somethingth floor at Work, my new colleagues were pleasant enough. Conversation wasn't all that different from what you hear in suburban kitchens.

I did my best to ingratiate myself with these glamorous, Work people. Was it my imagination or did they back, nervously smiling, into corners when I approached?

At lunchtime, I rode the elevator back to ground level to gulp petrol fumes in a concrete square lined with wind-burnt pot plants. A park, they called it.

I felt like a battery hen on the loose – uncertain what to do with my freedom. Still, it was great to be a Worker again. Someone who was worth something. Not just a bewildering glob of emotion people tried to mollify each year with Mothers' Day cards.

And the money, I thought, wandering past glossy shop windows. Once I'd paid for my work clothes, it would help keep the bank manager at bay.

It was then I noticed something odd about my reflection in the glass. There was something Alice in Wonderland about me.

I'd been far too interested in black rings earlier that day. My anxiety to catch the bus on time and make an impression on my new colleagues had been so overwhelming, I'd overlooked one small detail.

My shirt was inside out.

THE END

ABOUT THE AUTHOR

Helen Brown was born in New Plymouth, New Zealand, where her father managed the local gasworks. After an unremarkable school career, she followed her mother's footsteps into journalism. Helen went to Wellington Polytechnic School of Journalism then trained as a cadet reporter on *The Dominion*.

She moved to the UK in the early seventies to become a teenage bride and work on *The Woking Review* along with other magazines. When the couple returned to New Zealand to have two sons, Sam and Rob, she started writing regular columns about so-called ordinary life. She also wrote television scripts, current affairs for national radio and was a regular guest on TVNZ's *Beauty and the Beast*.

Her life was torn apart on 21 January 1983, when Sam, aged nine, was run over and killed. Amid the emotional devastation, a black kitten called Cleo was delivered to her doorstep. Cleo helped the shattered family take the first steps towards healing.

After Lydia's birth in 1985, the family moved to Auckland where Helen worked as a feature writer for the *Sunday Star*. *Don't Let Me Put You Off* is the first of eight books of collected columns. She was awarded a Nuffield Press Fellowship to Cambridge University.

Following her divorce, Helen met a handsome ex-army officer who was meant to be a one-night stand. They married in Switzerland and had a daughter, Katharine. Twenty-five years later, Helen and Philip are still together, surely creating the longest one-night stand in history.

Helen's memoir *Cleo* took the world by storm in 2010. A *New York Times* bestseller with two million copies sold, it's been published in more than seventeen languages. A major movie is in development.

The sequel, *After Cleo Came Jonah* (*Jonah* in the USA), was published in many languages and warmly embraced by readers and critics alike.

Her first novel *Tumbledown Manor* follows the adventures of a woman who reinvents herself after a disastrous fiftieth birthday. A bestseller in Australasia, it has also been released in the US, UK and Germany.

The third of her cat trilogy, *Bono The Rescue Cat,* has been released in the US and Australasia and translated into Russian, French and Chinese.

Helen lives in Melbourne, Australia, with Philip and their crazy, blog-obsessed cat Jonah. When she isn't writing, she enjoys making lemon slice with her adorable granddaughters, Annie and Stella.

Connect with Helen through:

www.helenbrown.com
or at facebook.com/Helen.Brown.International.Author

Printed in Great Britain
by Amazon

74070661R00097